KEPT IN MY HEART:

A Mother and Daughter

Early Childhood Asperger's Journey

By Tracey Ke

D1553427

Inspired by a true story.

"And Mary kept all these things,
reflecting on them in her heart."
(New American Bible Luke 2:19).

For My Family

You are my life,
my love, my inspiration,
my joy.

ACKNOWLEDGEMENTS

Special thanks go to Anna Epperson, my "GRAND" MOTHER, Mary Mifflin, Educator, Theresa Sanchez, Counselor, Evelyn Baughman, Mental Health Worker, Nicole Babcock, School Psychologist and all the many people who have shared our journey.

CHAPTER ONE

Noticing that we were late for bedtime again, I hurried to pick up my one year old daughter, Holly, lay her down on the bed and change her diaper. "Uh-oh!" she said, as her head bounced back on the mattress. "Money. Gone." Momentarily confused, I soon came to the conclusion that she had just swallowed a penny.

I called poison control to ask if she was in any danger. I kept remembering signs at the zoo about seals dying from coins that people had thrown in their exhibits. "She's not in any danger from a poison viewpoint," the worker responded. "I know this is going to sound extreme, but you need to take her to the emergency room and have them do an x-ray." I was wondering why an x-ray would be required for a swallowed penny. "They need to be sure that the penny made it down to her stomach and isn't still in her wind pipe," he explained. "Otherwise, she is at risk of the penny shifting from a vertical to a horizontal position while she's sleeping and cutting off her air supply."

I hung up the phone and announced to my husband, Ken, that we needed to take Holly to the emergency room. Once there, we explained to the doctor what had happened. "Well, why did you swallow that penny?" the doctor asked Holly. She did not respond. Once the doctor was able to determine that the penny had made it far enough down the digestive track, we were sent home with the motto, "This too shall pass."

When Holly was younger, I didn't think she had Autism and I had never even heard of Asperger's Syndrome or "High Functioning Autism." Like most mothers, I thought my baby was perfect. I just didn't know how really "special" she was.

I had heard about Autism and had even done some brief respite work with a seven year old girl with "classic" Autism. She was non-verbal and seemed to desire no social connections. While attending university to study Communicative Disorders, my part-time job as a respite worker involved babysitting this special needs child so her parents could get a break.

I had heard about babies who would cry when you picked them up and stop crying when you put them down. That was not the case with my daughter, Holly. She loved to be held and cuddled and rocked. She loved for me to sing and read to her. She stopped crying when I walked the floor with her.

One day, two year old Holly toddled over to her Papa and handed him the book "Are You My Mother" by P.D. Eastman. My Daddy, her Papa, was busy watching a baseball game and wasn't in the mood to read a children's book, but he couldn't turn his beloved granddaughter down cold. His joking personality took over. He pointed to the picture of the mother bird with a worm in its mouth. He told Holly, "See, this worm is getting ready to pull the bird down into its hole." Holly looked at him intently, waiting for the story. He turned to the first page and began reciting.

"This little piggy went to market," he "read." Holly looked at the picture of the mother bird on the egg and looked inquisitively at her Papa. She was standing next to his chair and leaning on the left arm rest. Papa turned to the next page.

"This little piggy stayed home," he continued. Holly looked at the picture of the egg. Then she looked at Papa. Papa was amused at the way she was studying him and trying to figure the situation out. Holly abandoned the left side of the chair and walked around back for a different perspective. She leaned against the right arm rest and waited for Papa to continue "reading."

"This little piggy had roast beef and this little piggy had none," Papa concluded. Well, that was his third strike. Holly was definitely on to him. She looked at him with disdain and snatched the book out of his hands. She immediately carried the book over to me where she knew it would be read correctly. Papa thought it had all been great fun!

I can't tell you when Holly first began using echolalia (repeated phrases), but I suspect it was at about three years of age. I don't know because I was too busy being her mom to think of it by its professional term. I never considered it echolalia until it was referred to as such by the speech-language pathologist who did her first formal evaluation. Later, others would argue about whether it was "true echolalia" (verbatim repetition of what was just said with no understanding of the meaning) or "delayed echolalia with communicative intent" (memorizing and repeating phrases, but using them meaningfully).

Regardless, I remember using it to my advantage. To get her to try new foods, I would quote *Green Eggs and Ham* by Dr. Seuss, "You don't like it, so you say! Try it, try it and you may! Try it and you may, I say!" And she would.

I also remember numerous incidents from the "delayed echolalia" that were only funny after being removed from the situation by time and space. Rather than learning vocabulary one word at a time and making her own word combinations, Holly would memorize phrases from books, videos or care-takers and try them out in conversation. One evening during dinner at a restaurant, Holly turned with gusto to the strangers at the table nearest us. She loudly quoted a line from the *Stuart Little* movie, saying, "Shoo! Get out of here! Scat!"

Another time, a lady from church told her, "You're such a sweet pea."

Holly replied, "You're such a pack rat." That was a line from a children's public television show (*Caillou*).

I remember one Thanksgiving when all the family gathered at my parents' house in the small community of Ponder, Texas for the holiday. Holly was three years old and I told them I was concerned that her language skills were not developing as they should. My big concern was that she was using single-word responses habitually and few word combinations. Imagine my surprise when later that same day, my sister, Holly's Aunt Amanda, told her, "Holly you're going to get chocolate pudding all over your pretty white dress."

Holly replied, "I really don't care." Imagine my surprise to hear that as her first sentence!

My brother, Richard, looked at me and said, "Be careful what you wish for; you might get it."

When I was away from Holly all day working full-time, I would come home and not understand where she was getting a lot of the things she was saying. However, when I stayed home with her, I would recognize chunks of her conversation as coming from *Dora the Explorer*, *Blue's Clues* or books we had read. I mentioned this trend to a fellow speech-language pathologist. She said, "In all my years of doing this work, I've never met a student who memorized sentences and tried them out in conversation."

Sometimes I would know Holly was quoting someone, but I couldn't remember who had said it. One such time, I asked her, "Who said that? Barney? Franklin (the turtle)? Big Bird?"

She answered each inquiry with "No, no, no," and then finally, "No, it was just a human."

When Holly was two, I was proud to hear people comment on how clearly she spoke. She would repeat phrases she'd heard with precise articulation. "Color on paper?" That was her reminder to herself not to color on walls, books, toys and anything else that would hold still long enough to be a canvas for her creativity. That didn't mean she didn't color on everything. She knew the rules, but she seemed to frequently "forget" them. When people were impressed with her clear articulation, my family members would say, "That's because her mom's a speech therapist." It was nice to think I was doing something right.

I'm sure she was using the jargon ("vocal play without meaning") at that time too, but it probably didn't seem so unusual for her young age. However, when the jargon continued past three years, people started asking, "What language is she speaking?" or "What's she saying?" (She wasn't saying anything; she was just making noises with no particular communicative intent.) When they thought I couldn't hear, people would snicker and say, "The funny thing is, her mom is a speech therapist." How quickly the story had changed!

In truth, I'm not sure how my mothering might have been different if I hadn't been exposed to clinical training before Holly was born. My interactions with her always seemed to be somewhat influenced by my professional role. A story was not just a story; it was the development of pre-literacy skills. Every conversation was an assessment of her current level and scaffolding to help her improve. I wavered between wondering why she was not developing according to the expected guidelines and vowing to put all the books away and stop being so "neurotic" about every developmental stage. "The problem is," I would reason with myself, "Holly hasn't read the books that explain how her language is supposed to develop. She's doing it her own way."

One afternoon, Holly was playing in her room of our new two bedroom apartment. I sat down on the carpet with her and tried to join in with the toys in front of her. Her language was developing. She was certainly creating meaningful communication this day that she had been unable to do a month ago. True, her conversations were littered with strings of unintelligible gibberish, but if you just ignored that you could make some sense of what she was saying.

"Duh-guh-dug-uh-dug-uh- is Holly Kennedy." She said, not too clearly.

"Did you say 'Holly's candy?' What candy?'" I asked.

"Holly Kennedy," came the clarifying response.

"Oh, Holly Kennedy. Yes, your name is Holly Kennedy and my name is Mommy Tricia Kennedy."

I began calling myself "Mommy Tricia Kennedy" for safety reasons. I could imagine Holly getting separated from me and someone asking her, "What's your Mommy's name?"

I knew she would respond, "Mommy" unless I taught her otherwise. However, if I taught her that my name was "Tricia" and not in fact "Mommy" then I could give up on her ever calling me anything other than my first name. So, I began presenting it as if my first name was Mommy and my middle and last names were Tricia Kennedy.

"Mommy Tricia Kennedy is Holly's Kennedy. Pocka my baby," Holly said.

"What?" I asked.

"Dumbo!" Holly abruptly changed topics, ignoring my question. "Look! Look at Dumbo!" I followed along and joined her attention with her Dumbo slippers. As a profession, we speech and language clinicians like to make a big deal over "joint attention." It is interesting, however, that as a young mother I was giving Holly credit for having joint attention, even when it was essentially me following along with whatever topic her attention jumped to next.

"Look at that little Dumbo!" Holly continued. "Look at that. Look at that Dumbo's dad."

"You can pretend this is Dumbo's dad," I started to explain, while holding the ant-eater Beanie Baby, "But, you know what? This isn't really an elephant."

"It's Dumbo's dad," she replied, matter of factly. I began to question my powers of persuasion. If I couldn't convince my two year old that an anteater is an anteater, how would I convince my future teenager to say "no" to drugs?

"This is an anteater. That long nose isn't an elephant's trunk; it's an anteater's nose," I explained.

"Duh-guh-dug-uh-dug-uh," she replied with unintelligible jargon.

"Are you trying to let them hug noses like they do in the *Dumbo* movie?" There was no response, verbally or through gestures. She didn't even look at me or acknowledge I had spoken. Our "conversations" were frequently one-sided due to Holly's non-responsiveness. Tenaciously, I repeated the question.

"No, not to watch the *Dumbo* movie," she said indignantly.

"I didn't ask you if you wanted to watch the *Dumbo* movie. I just said you were making them hug noses like that."

"Uh-oh!" she exclaimed.

"Uh-oh? What's wrong?" I asked. At times like these I frequently noticed that Holly and I could be in the same room and even participating in the same conversation without being in sync.

"Uh-oh!" she repeated, not providing any clarification.

"What? What's the matter?"

"Duh-guh-dug-uh-dug-uh ready to come out." She replied.

"What's ready to come out?" I slowly realized that I needed to turn my attention to the contents of the Dumbo slippers. "Something is in here," I said. "Goodness sakes, what'd you put in these slippers? There're all kinds of things in these slippers!" I pulled out various small toys before I pulled out Ken's watch. "This is Daddy's. He might be looking for that."

"Uh-oh! Uh-oh!" Holly said. I shook my head in wonder as I walked to go ask Ken if he had noticed his watch was missing.

CHAPTER TWO

When I was nine months pregnant with Holly, I was completing a clinical practicum at a local hospital, working towards completion of my Master's degree and working as a graduate assistant to bring in some money to help pay the bills. I had survived five months of "morning sickness," which was in reality twenty-four hours per day nausea only to have it return at the end of my pregnancy. The alarm clock would ring in the morning and I would think, "I can't keep up this pace." Trudging through my day, I would think, "I must be certifiably insane to be trying to do all this at once." Then I would meet other women who would reminisce about their pregnancies.

They would make comments such as:

"Your first pregnancy is the only time in your life when you get to be treated like a princess."

"My back hurt so much, all I could do was sit all day in the hot tub."

"Sometimes you just have to go take a nap."

Then, I would think, "They must be crazy too! When do I ever have time for a hot tub or a nap or to be treated like a princess?" The hot tub sounded especially inviting, but I didn't have access to one, even if I would have had time.

I put a poster above my desk at the Communicative Disorders department. It had an adorable baby with the caption, "Spit happens." I read, *Are You My Mother?* By P.D. Eastman everyday to my unborn Holly and talked to her and wrote to her in a baby journal. I rubbed my tummy and sang to her. Whenever things got especially stressful, I would find my old Cabbage Patch doll and smell the baby-powder scented hair and think, "Soon, baby will be here and all will be well."

On Thanksgiving, my brother, Richard and his family came to my parents' house from Florida. The next day, we all gathered at our one bedroom high-rise apartment in Dallas. Richard, my dad and Ken worked together to assemble the baby crib that Ken's grandmother had given us. So, after my baby shower, and over the next few weeks as more baby gifts began arriving, all baby-related items were stored temporarily in the empty crib. There was no baby in there and in a cramped one bedroom unit, we had few alternatives.

I'm told that some women become extreme neat freaks when they go through their "nesting instinct" just before they go into labor. I've heard of women scrubbing the cracks of their paneling with a toothbrush. My nesting instinct felt something like, "I'm going to have a baby and I have nowhere to put it!" I started yanking everything out of the linen closet to make room for baby clothes and diapers. Anything we didn't use regularly was thrown into boxes and stuffed in a corner or closet so that any functional space could be used to get the baby items out of the crib to make room for the baby.

It was around six o'clock in the evening when Ken looked at me with exhaustion and said, "We've been at this all day. Why don't we take a break and go get something to eat?"

I looked at him with the contempt that only a woman in pre-labor can understand. I said, "I have a feeling that once I leave this house, I'm not coming back until I bring a baby home with me and we are not ready! If you want food, you go and get it, but I am not leaving until I finish with this!"

Relieved to have my blessing to go, he left and returned about half an hour later with white paper bags from Dairy Queen. About five hours later, as I was in labor and checking into the hospital, the nurse asked, "What was the last thing you ate and when did you eat it?"

I was embarrassed to admit, "At about seven o'clock, I ate a cheeseburger, fries and a blizzard."

Holly was born the week after final exams. I appreciated her cooperation and timing with not coming two weeks earlier. However, she was only five and a half weeks old when the next semester started. I cried and said, "I don't want to leave her. I don't want to go back to school." University students are not eligible for paid maternity leave. It hurt Ken that he was unable to fulfill my wish of staying home, but he said honestly, "You have to go back. There is no way we can pay our bills without the money from your graduate assistantship."

Resigned that taking a semester off would not be an option, I called my mom on the phone. I cried and begged her to help with childcare. I couldn't bring myself to drop tiny newborn Holly off at a day care center. My parents agreed to be available to watch Holly any time during her first year when neither Ken nor I could be home. The hour long drive to our apartment, which was even longer if they hit Dallas traffic, frequently motivated them to just fold out our living room sleeper sofa and spend the night.

Issues of sleep disturbance with Holly have been going on for as long as I can remember. We were an easy target for blaming it on parenting. I was a college student throughout the pregnancy and newborn stages, and usually needed to be up late completing study and homework. Lights were on in the home well into the night and wee hours of the morning. Plus, I hated leaving her, so if we got to have a little quality time around midnight, whose business was it but ours?

When she was a newborn, the pediatrician said we were to put her in her bed with her eyes open so that she would learn to put herself to sleep. I tried to follow the doctor's advice, but none of us liked to listen to her cry. When my parents were staying with us, Papa especially did not approve of letting her cry it out. He would walk straight to Holly's crib in the corner of our bedroom, pick her up and carry her back to his favorite rocking chair. "You go on to sleep," he would say to me, "You have to get up in the morning. I can sleep all day."

Many nights, he would lay her down asleep and she would awaken a few minutes later. "Well, that didn't take," he'd say, as he went in and picked her up again. So, when she failed to develop healthy sleep habits, were we to think nature or nurture was the cause?

Even after Grandma and Papa stopped spending so much time staying in our apartment to help, we spent a lot of time visiting at their house. I frequently walked into the kitchen, carrying Holly in my arms. Papa spent a lot of time sitting at the head of the kitchen table, even when it wasn't meal time. He sat there to read the paper, drink coffee or even watch TV. That was his home base.

"Hey, Holly Clover!" He would call playfully to Holly as we entered the room. That nickname started on her first St. Patrick's Day when she wore a dress with four-leaf clovers all over it. Then, the nickname just stuck. Holly became her Papa's lucky four-leaf-clover. Sometimes she was in the mood for his brand of teasing and they would have a great time together. Other times she would just turn her head away and silently gaze in the opposite direction. Noticing that she was being somewhat rude in snubbing her Papa, I would turn around until she was facing him. She would then turn her head the opposite direction again.

"She can darn sure ignore you!" her Papa complained.

I felt guilty about leaving Holly as an infant, but I felt stuck. What else could I do? I just kept praying and moving closer to the bright light called graduation day. I told my mom, "Holly has sacrificed too while we have been working for these degrees. For nine months, she went to school with me. She's been exposed to so much college studying that I'm afraid her first word might be 'diadochokinesis,' only no-one will recognize it as a word! Not to mention the fact that for her first six months, she's put up with me being gone all day. She deserves for graduation day to be her day too!" So, my mom sewed a little black cap and gown for Holly. On graduation day, Mom, Dad and baby wore black caps and gowns.

Once our university days were over, I hoped to be able to stay home with Holly for awhile. I prayed that God would help Ken find a good enough job that we could live off of his income.

At first, he wasn't finding anything. He finally was hired by a small neighboring school district, teaching music for five hundred students in three elementary schools, kindergarten through fifth grade. It was clear that the main school principal didn't value the music program. She kept insisting that Ken attempt to teach music theory, even when Ken felt that her expectations were not appropriate for the younger grades.

The students started getting bored and frustrated and then began to engage in negative behaviors. Parents started calling the school saying that their children were not learning enough songs. Other parents complained that their children didn't even want to go to music anymore. Ken knew it was because of forcing them to learn too much music theory at too young an age, but the principal wouldn't approve his lesson plans without the music theory. The next year, the school board announced that the music program would be cut for financial reasons. The principal told Ken that perhaps he should look for a different kind of work. Ken was devastated.

I tried to be comforting and supportive. I said, "We won't tell anyone that your program was cut. Mama and Daddy are already planning to baby-sit Holly, once school starts. You can still leave the house at the same times you used to, but instead of going to work, you can go look for work. That way no one in the family will ever know the difference. Then, when you find a new job, we can just say that you quit that job because you found something better." In hindsight, I realize my protective instinct to conceal the whole matter, made Ken feel like being unemployed was somewhat like a "grave sin," too bad to even talk about.

Ken's confidence had taken a major blow. What he hoped would be a dream job, had turned into a nightmare. Not only was he let go, he was told to look for a different line of work. Then he felt like I was ashamed of him. It became difficult for him to even continue going through the motions of looking for work.

Even before the tumultuous emotional roller coaster ride from Ken's job began, it was clear that we would not be able to survive on his salary alone. Therefore, I reluctantly began my own job search. I applied at a private practice for speech and language therapy. The interview went well and the lady seemed interested in hiring me. Then the subject of sick days came up. She said, "I give one sick day every three months. That's four a year.

And you don't even have to take the whole day and you don't even have to be sick. You can take off half an hour to get your haircut."

I could tell she felt like she was being generous. However, thinking of my baby, Holly, at home, I couldn't see how it was going to work. "What would happen," I asked, "If my baby was running 104 degree fever two days in a row?"

She looked genuinely surprised, as she replied, "I don't know; we've never had that happen. I guess you would just owe me a Saturday or something." It was in that moment that I decided that job would not allow me to be the kind of mother I was determined to be. I then began to look seriously at working in the public school system myself.

It is interesting how God leads us in our lives. My earliest memories include wanting to grow up and become a mom. Then, I remember wanting to become a teacher, but by college age there seemed to be so many more glamorous professions to pursue. God used my strong desire to be with Holly as much as possible to lead me back to my early desire to be a teacher. I wanted to be home with Holly all the time, but if I had to work, it seemed the school schedule would be most compatible with motherhood.

I applied to a few local public school districts around the Dallas area. The district that I lived in accepted my resume, but I was told, off the record, that they were not known for hiring new speech and language personnel until after the school year started in September or October. I was offered a job in a nearby district and I accepted it. The salary was not enough to support the family. We still desperately needed Ken to find another job.

The school I was assigned to was an hour away from our apartment, in the opposite direction of Grandma and Papa's house. We chose to find child care near the school so that Holly would be as close as possible to me. We interviewed and found a lady who watched children in her home. She seemed kind and was neat to a fault. She was good for Holly, but it was difficult to pay her every week to do what I could only dream of doing, taking care of my baby all day.

It was not only emotionally difficult; it was financially difficult as well. Week after week, we were scrounging for the money to pay for child care. I would think of it in terms of, "We have to come up with enough money to bail Holly out on Friday."

Because the school was so far from home, Holly and I would have to get up early to get ready. I would nurse her and dress her, in addition to getting myself ready. It seemed we were always a few minutes late getting out the door. Then we would run into a few inevitable traffic jams or other unpredictable driving events. Since we drove through some rural areas to get to the small town school, we would sometimes have to stop for ducks crossing the road. It seemed we had a stressful start to each day.

After staying at school until five to keep up with the paper-work, I would go and pick up Holly from the baby-sitter. She would smile politely and make comments, such as, "I don't know how you do it. I couldn't do it. After my baby was born, I cried everyday at work; so I just had to quit."

"I wish I could quit and stay home with Holly," I would think, "But I can't pay my bills now. How could we survive without my paychecks?" Ken wrestled through several unsuccessful and unpleasant job transitions. He tried operating a camera for a morning news show, which required him to arrive at four o'clock in the morning and paid next to nothing. He tried selling cars and selling furniture. Since he was not a natural salesman and had not received formal training in sales, his commission-only jobs usually meant he worked all pay period only to have almost nothing to show for it on pay day.

This time period challenged my faith. Was this what all my hard work and toil had accomplished? I kept begging God to take care of us. I kept feeling discouraged knowing that, despite Ken's good intentions, his talents did not lend themselves easily into high paying positions. I began saying, "I wish I could just switch brains with you and let you be the speech-language pathologist and let me be the musician."

CHAPTER THREE

It was a bright, sun-shiny afternoon when I picked one year old Holly up from the sitter. The lady told me, "It's such a beautiful day; you should take her to the park when you get home."

I smiled politely and left without saying much. In my heart I was lamenting, "Doesn't she realize it's always dark by the time Holly and I get home?" We would have had to go to the park with a flashlight.

It bothered me that Holly was so little and had to spend two hours a day strapped into a car-seat. Sometimes she would sleep on the way home, making it impossible to get her to sleep again before midnight. We felt like we were doing what had to be done and we thought these issues would get resolved over time.

"Hug," Holly would frequently say. I recognized it as a request and I was happy to oblige. Then, I would bend down to kiss her cheek, but she would tuck her chin to her chest and I would kiss the top of her head.

One day, I heard Holly whining. Then, Ken complained, "Why won't you ever let me kiss you?" It was the first time that I had consciously realized that she never liked to be kissed on the face.

"Oh, wait a minute," I intervened. "She doesn't let me kiss her face either. I guess she doesn't like it. I always kiss her on the top of the head." He seemed less personally insulted, once he realized that she was giving us both equal treatment. It was a strange awareness for me to realize that I had so naturally accommodated her, without consciously noting her sensory issue of "tactile defensiveness."

There were early signs of her visual preferences as well. I remember one meal at a restaurant when she was one year old. At an adjacent table, there was a gentleman in a suit and tie dining alone. He was attractive enough to be a male model. Holly just stared at him as he tried to avoid looking at her and eat his dinner. I thought Holly had astonishingly good taste in handsome men. Dare I say she was demonstrating maturity beyond her age?

Holly learned some rote manners by age two. As the food was passed through the window at a drive-through, she would say, "Thank you." However, she didn't understand why her attempts failed when she tried to place her food order at the drive-through for the bank. As we were driving down the Dallas streets, she would look out her car window and see the golden arches and scream, "Combo!!!"

She was almost three years old when she came to visit me and newborn Shelly in the hospital. The muffled speaker sound could be heard, since the nurse was talking by intercom to the patient in the next room. Holly was sitting on top of me on the hospital bed while Ken held baby Shelly in the chair. Holly stopped, stared into space and listened intently. Then she ordered, "Uh, chicken nuggets, French-fries and Sprite."

As a two year old, Holly would lead me by the hand to share joint attention with whatever was on her mind. As she was leading me there, she would say, "Coming!" Suddenly, she stopped saying "coming" and began to combine unintelligible jargon "dug-udug-uh" with "going?" The vocal intonation matched with the way we would use our voices to ask, "Where are you going?"

If someone sneezed, Holly would say, "Bless you" when she was only two. Then we taught her the *Sneezing Song* by Jim Gill. The song repeats a loud, exaggerated sneezing sound at the end of each verse. After learning that song, she stopped saying, "Bless you" when someone sneezed and started saying, "Aaaah-Choo!"

It was difficult to capture Holly's early cuteness on video. Whenever she would see the video camera, she would stop what she was doing and stand grinning saying, "Cheese! Cheese! Cheese!"

I remember a road trip we took when Holly was about two. We drove about four hours to visit my sister, Amanda, at her home near Oklahoma City. Holly slept most of the way. When we arrived around midnight, Holly was wide-awake. Aunt Amanda suggested we put in a Disney video for Holly so that the rest of us could sleep. Holly quietly watched the video until the ending credits rolled. She came and woke me up. I was barely conscious when I took the first video out of the player and put in another Disney movie. I went back to sleep as Holly settled in for another show.

When the next show ended, Holly woke Ken up. He put in another show, which quieted her until she woke Amanda for the next show. This pattern continued until six o'clock the next morning! Amanda never again suggested putting in a movie to try to get Holly to fall asleep.

Holly had difficulty with the concept of sharing as a toddler and preschooler. Her understanding of the word "share" was "hand it over." If another child had a toy that she wanted, she would walk up to the child and loudly demand, "SHARE! SHARE! SHARE! SHARE!"

One Sunday, I carried her up the aisle with me as I went to Communion. She held out her hand to receive the Blessed Sacrament, which to her must have looked like some type of chip, cookie or cracker. The Eucharistic Minister blessed her by placing his hand on her head. The rest of the way back to our seat she was reaching over my shoulder, arm extended, shouting, "SHARE! SHARE! SHARE! SHARE!"

For Christmas, Aunt Amanda and Uncle Dan sent her a key chain with their pictures on it and a set of old keys. They knew that Holly was famous for taking our keys and hiding them from us so she could play with them. Giving her a set of her own seemed a great solution.

Noticing the photo key chain and wanting a closer look, Papa said, "Holly, let me see that for a minute." Holly responded by immediately leaning to one side, putting the keys under her diapered rump and sitting on them. They were her keys and there was to be no doubt about it.

That December, when Holly turned two, we took her to visit Santa at a local store. Secretly, it was Ken dressed up as Santa as a favor to our friends who owned the store. Holly did not recognize him and she had no desire to sit on his lap. We tried to place her on his lap just long enough to take the picture. In the picture, she was struggling with all her might to get away. She was also looking around at all of us, wagging her finger and saying, "No, no, no!"

Later that day, while we were still at the store, we were introduced to a friend of the store owner. The man looked at Holly and asked, "What's your name?"

"ME!" she responded.

"Me? Well, that's a very nice name!" the man chuckled.

When we went to put her in the car, she smiled widely at the dome light of the car. "Have you noticed she always does that when we put her in her car seat?" I asked Ken. "She thinks we're taking her picture."

Mothering a child with Asperger's is a different journey than the abrupt shock of learning that your child has a disability at birth. I believe that Holly's Asperger's was there from birth and that it was planned, by God, before she was even conceived. However, it was not visible when I wrapped her in a blanket at the hospital and buckled her into an infant seat for her first ride home.

The journey was like riding on an ocean of emotion. Rocky waves would stir feelings of concern that everything was not quite as expected. Is this within the wide range of "normal?" Am I just being paranoid, imagining things or over-reacting? One minute she is exceeding expectations, so how could there be a problem? Is it "wrong" or just "different?" Is she struggling because of something I did or didn't do or did she come hard-wired for this behavior? Then, the waters would calm and everything seemed smooth sailing for awhile, until the next storm hit.

When Shelly was born the next September, it seemed that Holly's world changed overnight. We had done everything we could think of to prepare her for the transition, but I knew she just wasn't getting it. I would try to get her to "feel the baby kick," but I don't think she ever felt it or sat still long enough to even begin to understand what we were talking about.

We read books like *The Berenstain Bears' New Baby* by Stan and Jan Berenstain, but she wasn't interested in those books. It was quite obvious that she didn't think the stories had any relevance to her life. She never acknowledged noticing that my tummy was getting big and round. She didn't notice I was sick or tired daily. Her little life seemed to be rolling on full speed ahead with few connections with what was going on with Ken or me.

Although I felt confident that God had spaced our children enough, when the reality of finding out I was expecting for the second time hit, I was a little nervous. We just weren't where we meant to be financially and I wasn't quite sure what was going on with Holly. We moved from our one bedroom unit in which Holly shared our room to a two bedroom apartment where Holly could share a room with the new baby. The transition proved to be difficult for Holly. She somehow seemed to feel that we were rejecting her by no longer sharing our room with her. I began to think, "I'm not sure I'm doing a good job supporting and parenting one baby. How am I going to handle two?"

Holly was still in diapers when I found out I was pregnant. Of course, the first thought was to hurry and help Holly grow up so she would be ready to be a big sister. However, as I read more books and articles, I learned that many toddlers who toilet train during their mother's pregnancy revert back to diapers once the new baby comes home. I thought, "So what's the point in stressing out over it now?"

I did a lot of praying and prompting Holly toward toileting, but I decided I would be patient and allow her to develop and mature at her own pace. I listened to the ladies from my church group who were fond of quoting, "If you baby your babies while they are babies, you won't need to baby them when they're not." They made it clear that those toddlers who were two or three years old were still truly "babies" and not ready to be pressured into growing up.

Another major shock wave wreaked havoc upon our family when I was four months pregnant with Shelly. The telephone rang at one in the morning. I answered. It was Amanda calling from my parents' house where she was visiting for Holy Week and Easter. Through her tears and shock, she said, "Tricia, Mama wanted me to call and tell you that the paramedics are here trying to revive Daddy."

My mind began swirling. My dad had experienced a heart attack nineteen years earlier when he was fifty. He had been a heavy smoker for more than fifty years. It was on-again, off-again, but more on than off. Before I had Holly, a doctor had sent us all into a tizzy by telling him, "I think you better go home and put your affairs in order because you don't have much time left on this earth." At that time, I had been terrified and devastated and cried gallons of tears, but then Daddy had gone to a cardiologist who performed an angioplasty, inserted a stint, and declared his health to be stable. Daddy had also recently been diagnosed with emphysema and was having more and more difficulty breathing.

Daddy had started saying, "I won't be around another year," but I firmly believed that it was depression. I was in absolute denial. I could not entertain the notion of losing him. I refused to participate in any such discussions.

"Daddy, don't talk like that," I would say.

All these thoughts raced through my mind along with the mental image of Mama, Amanda and her husband, Dan, there in my parents' house with paramedics surrounding Daddy attempting to save his life. The possibility of losing him was too terrible a concept for me to accept. "It's going to be okay," I said, "Just pray!"

"I don't know," Amanda said, "He looked really white."

"Just pray!" I demanded. I was irrationally annoyed that she was suggesting that there could be any outcome other than a positive one. "I'll be there as soon as I can."

"Okay, okay," she said. "They're taking Daddy in the ambulance. Dan and I will drive Mama to the hospital. Carol will meet you here." Richard was still in Florida due to work obligations. Carol, his wife, was staying with her parents in Dallas.

I hung up the phone. "Ken, I have to go. They're taking Daddy to the hospital. He's had a heart attack."

"Do you want me to go with you?" he asked.

"No. Then we'd have to wake Holly and take her with us. There's no time for that. I've got to go. You stay here with Holly."

Remembering that Daddy had never been baptized, I grabbed the bottle of Holy Water from Lourdes, France that Amanda had given me. I was expecting to arrive at the hospital and see Daddy sitting up in a hospital bed. I imagined how we would all talk about what a close call it had been and how scared we all were. I would bring up the idea of baptism and I hoped he wouldn't refuse. My firm belief was, "Nothing could happen to anyone in my immediate family because God knows I couldn't handle it."

Alone in the car, on the way to Mama and Daddy's house, I sang the familiar hymns that we had just sung the night before at the church Lenten mission. I pulled into the driveway and rushed into the house. I arrived at the house before Carol. I wanted to rush to Daddy's side, but I had promised to meet her there. I rushed around the house trying to be helpful, denying my true feelings of helplessness. I saw Daddy's false teeth. "He's going to want to eat later," I thought. "He'll need those." I put them in a plastic bag, feeling like a thoughtful daughter.

Armed with Holy Water and dentures, I jumped into Carol's car as soon as she pulled into the driveway.

"I'm so scared," she said,

"He's going to be okay." I reassured. "Let's pray the Rosary on the way."

We reached the hospital and hurried in. We were going down seemingly endless hallways as fast as we could walk.

"Are you all right?" Carol asked, noticing my heavy breathing.

"Well, I'm as all right as you are," I commented.

"You're not going to go into early labor are you?" She asked.

"No. Let's just hurry up and get there."

Finally we reached the desk at the emergency room and told them who we were there to see. Someone said, "Come right this way" and led us toward a room. Later, Carol said that she read the sign "conference room" on the door and feared the worst. I never noticed the sign. I walked in still expecting to see Daddy.

Instead, I saw Mama crying and leaning on Amanda. Dan broke eye contact with me and looked at the floor. Amanda slowly shook her tear-soaked face. Carol broke into tears immediately and the hospital personnel slunk out of the room without saying a word to Carol or me. They had already delivered the solemn news to Amanda, Dan and Mama.

I still wasn't accepting it. Okay. Obviously, it was bad news, but it couldn't be final. His condition must be critical, but they'll pull him through. He has to come through this. He has to be okay. I can't lose him. It's not possible.

I walked closer to Mama and she threw her arms around me and buried her head in my shoulder. "I can't go on!" She sobbed.

"Oh, yes you can!" Amanda demanded. She had just faced the loss of one parent and she was determined not to lose our remaining one.

Finally, the stunned realization was smothering me. Daddy was gone. The nightmare was upon us. It couldn't be, but it was. We all hugged and cried. Eventually, we turned to leave the conference room. Mama had asked for a rosary and directions to the chapel. As I walked through the doorway, I heard Amanda say in sorrow, "And he donated his body to science so we can't even bury him."

I was thinking, "How is she, in this moment, even remembering that he donated his body to science and what comfort would there be in burying him anyway?" I wanted to find a "Customer Comment Card" and object to the entire situation. Stop. Rewind. Delete. Re-record!

Carol handed me her cell phone. "You better call Ken and tell him to bring Holly. Then I've got to call and tell Richard."

I dialed home. When Ken answered, I took a no-questions commanding tone. "They weren't able to save Daddy. I need you to get Holly up, get her dressed and bring her here right away!"

"Oh, Baby," Ken said, "I'm so sorry."

I wasn't ready for sympathy. I didn't know what I needed from him or anyone at that point.

"Just get here right away. This is the last time Holly will get to see her Papa."

Soon after, Ken arrived with our bleary-eyed two year old Holly who had been awakened in the middle of the night to find me gone and her Daddy rushing to dress her and take her to the hospital. Not knowing how to tell her what was happening, he just told her that he was bringing her to me.

I carried her into the room where her Papa's body lay on a gurney, covered with a sheet up to his shoulders. Mama was there with her head upon his still chest. She started to leave the room, then turned back to grasp his feet which were wrapped in the white sheet.

I kept thinking, "This can't be happening. This isn't real. This is not my dad." I had Holly there though and I knew this was my only opportunity to let her see to believe. I carried her closer and said, "Holly, Papa's gone to live with Jesus now."

Amanda began to sob more, "Oh, don't say that!" She complained. I don't know what else she thought I should say. It was the gentlest way I could think to explain it. It would be more than a month before I could bring myself to say that he had "died" or was "dead" or had "passed away."

When I called work in the morning, to tell them I wouldn't be coming in, I cried as I told my principal, "My dad had a heart attack. I went to the hospital, but it was too late. He didn't make it."

I stopped worrying so much about toilet training at that point. Holly and I were grieving a significant loss and babying her was something we both needed. It seemed that all of life's rules had changed anyway. What I thought would never happen just happened. I now realized that I wasn't immune to bad things happening to me or anyone I loved. My mind kept replaying the line of the REM song, "It's the end of the world as we know it." My thoughts were like a broken record; I could not continue to the lyric "…and I feel fine."

The next few nights, the family gathered at Mama's house until well past midnight. The house seemed so big and empty, even with all the family visiting. It also seemed scary; the world no longer felt safe.

Ken drove himself home around ten. He was starting a new job selling cars and needed to get up and get to work on time and make a good impression. Holly and I stayed another couple hours. I wasn't ready to leave the family gathering yet. Finally, around midnight, I reluctantly said that Holly and I had better be getting home.

"Is that apartment complex you live in safe for the two of you to go home alone this late?" Richard asked. "Is the parking lot well-lit?"

I had felt quite safe back when I thought all was right with the world. Now, I was a little nervous, but I didn't want to inconvenience anyone by making them drive us home. "We'll be okay." I said.

We drove and pulled into the closest space in the parking lot to our apartment. I opened the back car door and unbuckled two year old Holly from her car seat. Above us were the trees, a streetlight, the moon and a star-lit sky. Carrying Holly quickly to our apartment, I was stunned when she stared into the night sky and questioned, "Papa? Up there?"

I immediately looked up. Unable to see anything supernatural myself, I wondered, "Can you see him?" Then I almost hated to bring her indoors feeling like I was abruptly ending their visit.

It was during this early grief period that my mother shared a simple, favorite prayer: "My Jesus, I trust in you."

The prayer was brief, but meaningful, so I began reciting it frequently. I would say it as one of my morning prayers and night prayers and driving down the road. One day, as I was driving, I rattled, "My Jesus I trust in you."

By way of response, I heard my dad's voice in my mind saying, "Oh really?" Instantly, I realized that I was a long way from trusting God's will in my life. I hadn't trusted God's will in his timing about when to bring my daddy home. In this area, and in many others, I thought I had a better idea for how things should be. I do not know whether my dad spoke to me from heaven, or if it was some part of my subconscious mind, but I recognized that, for a person of faith, I was clinging to a lot of fear and doubt.

CHAPTER FOUR

A few months later, I saw a friend from church. "How are you feeling?" she asked me. She was inquiring about the pregnancy. After about a month of grief, everyone assumed that was ancient history and no longer asked about that. I quickly learned that social norms involved putting on a happy face.

"Oh, always tired," I said with a smile, not sure whether or not I should go into more details of every pain and discomfort.

"And how are you doing?" She asked Holly. Holly just stared at her, saying nothing in reply. "I hear you're going to be a big sister!" she said. Again, Holly just stared at her, as if the words were from a foreign language. "Does she ever talk?" She asked me.

"Oh, you'd be surprised," I chuckled. "Sometimes we can't stop her, but it's totally unpredictable. She follows her own ideas, not necessarily ours." I smiled, knowing that my friend probably didn't understand, but she would stay within the framework of polite small talk. I didn't have any better words to explain it anyway. One minute people would think Holly was mute and the next minute they'd be amazed at her knowledge and eloquence.

My friend decided to give one last-ditch effort to communicate with Holly. "Are you going to have a new baby at your house?"

"No!" Holly said, loudly and emphatically. Startled, my friend and I looked at each other with wide eyes. She kept looking at me, waiting for some comment or reaction.

"I'm not really sure what that was all about," I shrugged.

"Denial?" she asked.

"I guess we'll soon find out," I replied. We said our goodbyes and parted ways. As I watched her get in her car and drive off, I doubted that she was envying me for my situation.

A couple months later, I got up and dressed myself and Holly. I drove her to the babysitter and dropped her off. I drove myself an hour and a half to a Speech-Language Pathology conference in Sherman, Texas. I was days away from my due date. At my last appointment, I asked my doctor if I was okay to make the trip.

"You're not showing any signs that you're going to do anything," he began, indicating that my exam didn't show that labor was imminent. "As long as you take your own car so that you are free to leave if you need to, you should be fine. I have patients who live that far away and they drive themselves to the hospital in time."

All day long I kept having what I was calling "Braxton Hicks contractions." People would see my bulging tummy and ask when I was due. When I told them, they looked panicked and asked, "And you're here?"

I stayed the whole day and drove back home to Dallas. I picked up Holly at the babysitter's. My mom had been scheduled for sleep apnea surgery that day, so I drove to her house to see if she was home. She wasn't, but I went in and called Amanda for an update. She had come to town for Mama's surgery. As I was talking to Amanda, my water broke.

I called Ken at work. "My water just broke."

"I'll be right there!" He sounded so excitedly frenzied that I worried he might wreck on the way.

I called Amanda back and asked her to watch Holly. Amanda and Ken arrived at Mama's house at about the same time. We left Holly at Grandma's house with Aunt Amanda and we drove and checked into the hospital. Four hours later, Shelly was born.

Holly was strongly attached to me and never imagined that another person could share that "daughter role." For Holly, it wasn't just that I was "her mother" in the biological or genetic sense. It was possessive. She believed she owned me. She could not have been more dismayed at the idea that I would share my love with another daughter than I would have been if Ken announced that he had decided to share his love with another wife. Of course, social norms dictate that polygamy is wrong, but it is perfectly natural and normal for parents to have more than one child. However, Holly was not born with that intrinsic rule book. When she saw me with the baby in the hospital and then she had to go home and the baby got to stay, I hurt for her.

I have never seen such a look of betrayal as the first time Holly saw me nurse the new baby. Nursing was something that she remembered that she and I had shared. She had never seen me do that with anyone else and she never imagined that she would.

From her perspective, it was suddenly and without warning that all the adults she loved and trusted changed their expectations of her. She was no longer the darling grandbaby of the family; she was expected to behave like a big sister. I felt enormous pressure to protect her. They say a mother's instinct is to protect her newborn child, but I knew Shelly was fine. Everyone was fawning over her. I would hear people get harsh with Holly and I would think, "She's not acting any differently than she did last week."

After blaming ourselves for getting Holly off to a poor start with her sleep habits, we tried multiple times in multiple ways to go back and make it right. There were nights we tried to "just leave her in her room," but by that time she was capable of getting out of bed by herself. She would scream, yell and pound on the bedroom door. We were living in a rented apartment and property damage was one concern. Worry that a well-meaning neighbor might call protective services was another concern. Soon, however, Holly learned to manipulate all door knobs and "child-proof" locks so that the only way to contain her in a room was to hold her or hold the door.

I remember thinking that we didn't want to repeat the same mistakes with our second child. The girls were sharing a room, so we thought we'd just leave them both in there. There was some concern about what Holly might do when she was unsupervised with her newborn sister, so I always listened closely to the baby monitor and wished it had video capability. Shelly was probably about 3 months old, not even old enough to do much babbling, when she was crying in her crib. Her loud unintelligible cries frustrated Holly who began coaching her, "Stop it! Say 'Mommy!' Say 'Mommy!'"

One afternoon during Lent, I read the *Children's Way of the Cross,* about Jesus' suffering and death, to three year old Holly. At first, I had to fight for her attention, but then she got interested and was engaged throughout the reading. There was one picture where Jesus was being nailed to the cross. One hand was already nailed and the other hand dangling down. Holly pointed to the dangling hand and said it was "supposed" to be on the cross. I was, on one level, appalled by her comment since it expressed the polar opposite of my feelings. However, I recognized that she had seen the visual image of Jesus on the cross countless times, but had never before seen Jesus partially on the cross. From her visual frame of reference, that made the picture "wrong." I recognized that she was experiencing the picture in a completely different way than I was.

I explained that the people were being very mean to Jesus when they nailed him to the cross and that they hurt him a lot. I pointed to the picture of the nail in the other hand. She looked like she was going to cry. She was visibly upset on a deep, emotional level. Then, we read through the end of the story, which included the resurrection. We sang the song "My Jesus is alive, alive forevermore..." She sang with gusto and said, "Yea!"

Just before Easter, a local Catholic school did a re-enactment of the Way of the Cross. We took Holly. It began with, "The First Station: Jesus is condemned to death." As a group, we walked a distance of about half a block while pushing seven month old Shelly in the stroller. We stopped for the young actors to portray "The Second Station: Jesus carries His cross." Holly didn't seem to be paying much attention at all and I wondered why we had bothered bringing her. She happily walked along, as if out for a stroll. She attempted to socialize with the people around us.

Near the end of the presentation, after we had walked several blocks, the youth group depicted "The Eleventh Station: Jesus is nailed to the cross." Holly watched intently and loudly and dramatically exclaimed, "Poor Jesus!" In that moment, it seemed that it all became real to her.

I heard the stranger behind us say, "That made it worth coming, right there."

Holly was unusually quiet and solemn, as we walked by the presentations for the twelfth, thirteenth and fourteenth stations: "Jesus dies on the cross. The body of Jesus is taken down from the cross and Jesus is laid in the tomb." We had to remind Holly that the story did not end there.

"Jesus died again!" she complained bitterly.

"No," I reassured her. "They were just acting out a play to remind us about when Jesus died." As the words were coming out of my mouth, I imagined that Holly was probably wondering why they would want to remind us of that. "Jesus was willing to die for us because He loves us and He wants us to go to heaven to be with him forever, but he is alive forevermore. He will never die again." We sang the "Alive Forevermore" song again and she seemed to be comforted.

I was painfully aware that Holly was not "getting" things. I knew she needed my one on one attention so I would try to get the baby to sleep so that I could give Holly what she craved. Finally, I would get Shelly to sleep and start walking to the baby's bassinette when Holly would loudly demand, "Baby in bed!" and try to pull her out of my arms, of course, waking her up. Then, they were both screaming and crying again. It was then that I noticed the echolalic behavior, although I didn't call it that.

"Holly!" I whispered firmly.

"Holly!" she echoed back in the same firm whisper.

"Be quiet!" I scolded.

"Be quiet!" she repeated.

"The baby is sleeping!" I tried to explain.

"The baby is sleeping!" My own words ricocheted back to me through Holly's voice. It was enough to drive a young mother crazy.

At that time, when Shelly cried, Holly would laugh. It was quite unnerving. We finally decided that Holly was just fascinated thinking, "It's alive!"

So many nights, I was struggling with Holly and Shelly both being awake. Holly fought her own sleep and woke the baby by being loud and active. Ken rarely had any luck getting either of them to sleep. He would get frustrated and then I felt like I was dealing with three unhappy campers. I developed the habit of letting Ken sleep while I tried to coax the girls back to sleep myself. I would think, "I miss my daddy! I wish Papa were here to say, 'Go on to bed; I'll take care of this.'" Then I would think, "If he could even get one of them to sleep, I'd at least have a chance with the other one!"

I knew I could no longer handle it alone, when, as a full-time speech therapist, I started getting kids on caseload who were born the same year as Holly. The first such child seemed perfect in every way, except she was referred to me because she couldn't say her "f" sound. I remember thinking, "It's crazy for me to be leaving Holly with a babysitter who watches soap operas all day so I can teach this girl 'bite your lip like this, say /fffff/' and then go home to hear Holly saying "Duh-guh-dug-uh-dug-uh pocka my baby."

"Ken, I am really worried about Holly and I think I need to be home with her." I began to voice my concerns. It was a difficult subject to bring up.

Ken was miserable with his sales job and we were still struggling to survive paycheck to paycheck. He would come home nightly and complain about how terrible his work environment was. I was in no mood to be empathetic. I had lost my dad, I had a newborn baby and I had no idea what was going on with Holly.

"I'm going to quit my job!" Ken fumed as he walked through the door one night.

"Fine! Then, I'm quitting mine too!" I raged back. Ken turned quickly and glared at me. It was quite obvious that they were mutual idle threats. Neither of us could abruptly quit our jobs, despite how much Ken loathed his job or how strongly I wanted to be home with Holly.

I gradually began to talk to Ken about my concerns and explain that I thought Holly needed to be evaluated. It was indeed humbling to be so unsure of her needs. At first, I didn't call any of the people I had gone to school with. I didn't want them to know that I didn't have all the answers for my own child. Likewise, I didn't confide in any of my professional colleagues. I didn't want them to lose respect for me as an educator.

I did give notice that I would not be returning to work the next school year. Holly needed me. That was an act of blind faith. I read in a Christian publication that "God will provide the means for a man to support his family except in the case of a physical disability leaving him unemployable." I told Ken that I believed in him and I trusted him. My paychecks would continue throughout the summer. In that time, I knew he could find something that would allow me to stay home and help Holly. I promised to follow him to the ends of the earth if that is where his job search led us.

CHAPTER FIVE

I happened to be living in one school district and working in another. So, I quietly called the school district in which we resided and requested a speech and language evaluation for Holly. The Speech-Language Pathologist called me back and asked me about my concerns. By the end of our brief conversation, she decided that a School Psychologist and Social Worker should be involved in the evaluation as well.

Having Holly evaluated began the process of bringing private concerns into "public light." We were asked about her sleep habits, her eating habits, her development, her TV watching. It felt a little like being on trial for our parenting habits. However, I knew that it was the only way to get Holly the help she needed.

Holly had her initial special education evaluation when she was three and a half and Shelly was eight months old. The evaluation team determined that Holly was "developmentally delayed."

I was able to observe the evaluators interacting with her. I remember the School Psychologist asked her if she was a girl or a boy. First, she ignored his question completely. After he persisted in asking, she repeated verbatim, "girl or boy." I remember thinking, "Oh no! I didn't think to teach her that."

From that day on, I would say things like, "How's my girl?" whenever I thought of it. There were many items on their evaluation that she could not successfully demonstrate or answer. For each one, I would scold myself inside. I didn't teach her that either (ex. Her last name, how to ride a tricycle, how to poke and squeeze Play-Doh with her fingers).

There were things she did well during the evaluation. She matched colors, named colors, named shapes, labeled objects, and described actions currently occurring. She also engaged in brief verbal interactions with the adult evaluators. She "separated easily" from me, seemed to enjoy herself and didn't want to leave the colorful toy-filled environment.

The "separating easily" was true for more than just the evaluation sessions. Holly had a tendency to separate a little too easily at times. It's not that we weren't bonded. There were plenty of times when I was dropping her off at the babysitter that I would have to peal her screaming body off of me and make a narrow escape. However, when she was feeling in control of the situation, she had no problem separating.

I recalled one Sunday after church when my little toddler began to wander away from me. My psychology textbooks had taught me that there is a certain distance that a child will be willing to explore before rushing back to the comfort of mother. I decided to watch closely to judge how far that distance was for Holly. When she cleared the midway point toward the exit, I decided that distance was "Egypt" and I quickly hurried to catch up with her before she could escape. Holly developed a habit of disappearing into the crowd after the church service ended. Ken and I always said we could intensely relate to Mary and Joseph when they lost the child Jesus in the temple.

I also remembered another time when Holly was even younger, maybe nine months old. We went to the grocery store and the clerk (a stranger) started sweet talking with my pretty baby. Holly held out her hands for the clerk to hold her. The clerk's heart melted and I reluctantly allowed her to hold my baby for a moment. Then I held out my hands and said, "Okay, Holly, it's time to go." Holly turned her back on me in favor of remaining with the unknown woman holding her. Now the clerk was sure she was the sweetest baby in the world, but I was more than a little annoyed. "Enough is enough!" was my thought as I snatched my reluctant baby back and carried her to the car.

The results of her multidisciplinary evaluation found Holly to be unable to describe or talk about past or future events. Her language was entirely in the "here and now." She had absolutely no interest in asking or answering "why" questions. When I thought about that, I remembered how most three year olds drive their parents crazy with constant questions of "Why? Why? Why?"

The evaluators noted that Holly preferred to play alone and did not seem to notice there was another child present. Although, she did sometimes watch him play and try out his toy as soon as he left it. Surprisingly, she did not approach him on that day and demand, "SHARE! SHARE! SHARE!"

When the team recommended an Early Childhood program, I couldn't imagine my three year old "baby" going to school. The school building itself was large and intimidating and, since I had a newborn at home, Holly rode a big, yellow bus to school. At her initial Individualized Education Program (IEP) team planning meeting, I was apologetic to school staff about all the self-help skills she still needed to master. We had been working on them, but we were hoping for two more years to get them accomplished. She still was eating in a high chair to limit food/drink spillage and escaping from the table. She was still in diapers and our numerous efforts toward potty training had not been met with enthusiasm or success. We were told not to worry since these teachers had been potty training several children per school year over multiple years. They were the experts.

Holly was excited on her first day of school. She even woke up and let us help her get dressed, without a struggle. We took pictures of her in her cute little school uniform that Grandma had altered to fit a three year old and her book bag that looked as big as she was. Grandma had even dressed Holly's Cabbage Patch doll in a matching school uniform.

I was concerned about nap time at school. "How is this going to work?" I asked my mom. "Holly never falls asleep without me being there." We packed a silky blanket and a small Pooh Bear toy in her backpack and hoped for the best.

We drove Holly to school on the first day. She navigated straight toward the toy kitchen in the early childhood classroom. She was so happy playing with the new toys, she barely noticed me as I told her goodbye. The teachers and paraprofessionals said, "It looks like she'll be fine."

As I was leaving, I glanced around the room at the other students. They looked strikingly different from Holly. Their disabilities were not so hidden. I saw children engaged in hand-flapping, a child confined to a wheelchair being fed by a nurse, a student with Down's syndrome and a child screaming and hitting himself. I began questioning whether or not we had made the right decision.

I called my mom as soon as we got home. I described the scene to her. "Could that possibly be where Holly belongs?" My mom assured me that it would be okay and that Holly would just learn empathy for the students with higher needs.

After lunch on that first day, I received a phone call from the school. The classroom nurse explained to me that Holly had been doing fine until it was nap time. They said she then began to scream and cry and try to escape.

"I was worried about that." I said, "It is always extremely difficult to get her to sleep. If you want me to, I can come get her, but it will probably just teach her that if she cries at naptime she gets to go home."

"So, she does this at home too?" the nurse asked.

"Yes."

"Well, if she resists falling asleep at home, then, of course, she would resist it here. We'll just go ahead and keep her here."

"Okay. Call me back if you want me to come." I hung up the phone and my heart sank, knowing that Holly was sad and calling for me and all I could do was wait.

There was another topic of concern. I told Ken, "Your dad would freak out if he ever saw her class."

"Okay." Ken replied nonchalantly. "We just won't tell him."

"It's not that easy. We can't 'not tell him' that she's going to school. Holly will tell him about her new school and then he'll say, 'Why didn't you tell me?'"

"What do you suggest?" He asked.

I thought about a plausible cover story. "We'll just tell him that she's involved in a special program for three year olds at that elementary. It's not lying and it's all he needs to know."

So, when the time came, that's what we told him. His response was, "It's not Head Start, is it?

You don't want her in Head Start! What a messed up program that is!"

"It's not Head Start," we confirmed. In my mind, I was thinking, "If you only knew!"

One day, I picked Holly up from school. "How was your day?" I asked.

"Good. We ate chicken and mashed potatoes and gravy." I found it odd that every time I asked about her day she recited the lunch menu. The rest of her school experience was a bit of a mystery to me. I had to refer to the written "Preschool Daily Report" for clues.

Mrs. Turner provided a checklist, which included Holly's mood, whether or not she participated, whether or not she ate lunch, diaper/toileting, whether or not she attended speech therapy and whether or not she took a nap. She also sent home copies of the lesson plans for the week. Between the lesson plans and the daily report, I could usually find a way to bridge the gap between school and home. I might be able to sing a song they sang at school or read a story or play a game related to the theme of the week. If I had not had the written work from school, I would have been clueless.

One day, Holly woke up saying she had a broken leg. We couldn't see anything wrong with her leg so we started getting her up and ready for school. In the bathroom she said, "It's almost time for me to go to heaven." Later in the day she fell and scraped her knee. She repeated, "Look at the blood. It's almost time for me to go to heaven."

One of the other moms asked, "Did I hear that right?"

"She has a flair for the dramatic," I commented.

Prior to entering school, Holly just wasn't interested in learning about letters. I would sing the alphabet song while pointing to the letters and she would walk away. Once the letters were introduced in the school setting, her interest was ignited. Then, she came home and wanted to sing letter songs and point to letters. She began to notice letters everywhere in the world around her.

We stopped by to pick up Ken's asthma medicine at the pharmacy. Holly noticed the letters in the store's name and began calling out, "P-P-P-P!" Onlookers stared at us, believing that she needed the rest room. Then, she pointed to an alphabet chart and said, "'Z' is for 'bee:' zzzzz!"

After just two days of preschool, I left Shelly at home with Ken and I went to pick up Holly. Mrs. Turner met me at the door. "She didn't test well, did she?" She asked.

"What do you mean?" I inquired.

"I don't usually get kids like Holly in my class. She's too bright. I'm not sure she belongs in my class."

"Well, the people who evaluated her seemed to think she needed to be here. I guess I'd like to give it more time."

By the next week, the story was changing. "Holly won't answer any direct questions," the teacher told me.

"What do you mean?"

"When it's free time, and the other kids are off playing with the toys, Holly goes to our lesson wall and names all the letters, and the colors, and the shapes, but at circle time, when I ask her to name one of those things, she just sits there and won't say a word. Today, I tried to motivate her with stickers so I gave a sticker every time anyone gave a correct answer. The other kids were covered head to toe in stickers, but Holly never got one because she never answered a question."

I looked down at Holly to see if it had been a frustrating day for her, or if she seemed sad to be the only one in the class who didn't earn a sticker. She seemed entirely unaffected. Of course, Holly wasn't a big fan of stickers anyway. She never liked them sticking to her. When the doctor's offices gave her stickers, she always stuck them to me, or to a wall, if no one was looking.

When I received Holly's first progress report, it contained both positive comments and areas of concern. It detailed the goals and objectives for which Holly was making progress. The comment that struck me the most was, "The one rule not followed by Holly is participation during lessons." I wondered why Mrs. Turner was so certain that Holly was "breaking a rule" rather than demonstrating a skill-deficiency.

CHAPTER SIX

One evening at home, Holly got a little rowdy, was flailing her arms and legs and accidentally kicked me in the mouth. "Now, Holly, that hurt! You need to tell me you're sorry," I told her emphatically. Holly began struggling to get away from me and made no verbal response, other than whimpering. "Say, 'Sorry, Mommy!'" I coached. Still no response. I continued prompting and persuading until I realized that there was not going to be an apology. In fact, by demanding one I had made the situation worse. At first she had only neglected to apologize. Now she had refused to apologize. There was no way I could force her to say it.

I decided to cut my losses and end the battle, but Ken hadn't followed my train of thought. He began badgering Holly. "You need to tell Mommy you're sorry! You hurt her! Say you're sorry!" The tension in the room was rising and things were not getting better. There was no resolution in sight.

"She's not going to say it, so just forget it!" I told Ken. He gave me a look of confusion. Weren't we correct in insisting that she apologize? Reluctantly, he followed my lead. We backed away from Holly and began quietly talking amongst ourselves.

A few minutes later, Holly cried out loudly, "But I don't want to hurt Mommy!" In her mind, there was some strange connection between saying sorry and hurting me. Perhaps she thought that you only say sorry if it was on purpose. At any rate, her refusal to apologize had been out of love.

After a few weeks of school, Mrs. Turner decided to begin the potty training. It was a disaster.

50

I noticed that Holly's attitude toward school had abruptly changed. Instead of being excited to go to school, she began refusing to cooperate with getting ready.

"Holly, it's a school day," we would tell her.

"No, it's NOT a school day!" She would shout.

"We have to get ready. The bus will be here soon."

"The bus will NOT be here soon!"

"Well," I analyzed, "her language skills include proficiency in using negatives in sentences and she could teach motivational seminars about positive thinking and telling it like you want it to be, but why doesn't she want to go to school anymore?"

I went to the school to talk to her teacher. "She is the most stubborn child I have ever had in my sixteen years of teaching. And you are going to have to deal with that her whole life," she told me. A vision flashed through my mind of Holly dressed in a beautiful, red Miss America gown with a white sash draped from shoulder to waist. Instead of "Miss Congeniality" the sash said, "Most Stubborn." I didn't have anything nice to say, so I stood in stunned silence.

"We put her on the potty and she doesn't do anything," the teacher began explaining. "Then, five minutes later, she wets her diaper. She is controlling that. So, I've started putting her in time-out every time she wets her diaper."

So, the potty training had become a power struggle and that's why Holly no longer wanted to go to school. "I'm concerned," I began, "with the fact that Holly doesn't want to come to school anymore. She's only three. She has a lot of years of school ahead of her. I don't want to teach her to hate school before she even gets to kindergarten. So, if there's anything we can do at home to help...."

"You know what will help the most?"

"What?" I asked expectantly.

"Prayer." This was a teacher who had seen me at church and knew that I was a person of faith. Of course I pray for Holly, but that was not the response I expected when I asked a teacher what we could do at home.

She continued. "I have put Holly on my prayer circle and I have asked the group to pray for very specific things for her. I have asked them to pray that the spirit of uncooperativeness will leave her."

"Does she think my daughter is possessed?" I wondered.

"And another thing," Mrs. Turner continued. "I would take her to your priest and I would insist that he do the Sacrament of Anointing. I took my kids to a healing service and they didn't want me to bring them forward, but who are they to say that physical healings are more important than mental?"

My mind whirled at what I had heard. "I am sending Holly every day to a place where she is completely misunderstood," I began thinking. "Maybe the speech therapist has a better understanding of what is in fact going on with Holly," I hoped.

As Holly and I were leaving the building, we saw the speech therapist in the hall.

"Hello, Little Miss," she said to Holly. I assumed that meant she didn't remember her name. Then she looked at me. "Little Miss can speak and very clearly, but it's only at her choosing!" She assessed.

My hopes were entirely deflated. "Of course she can speak clearly," I thought. "I never said she had an articulation disorder. If her professional opinion is that Holly is fine if she chooses to be fine, then it doesn't sound like she has much planned to help her."

"I hope you reported that teacher to the principal," a friend told me, as I related the experience. Running to complain to the principal was not my style. I wanted Mrs. Turner to like me and to like Holly.

I didn't want her to think, "Here comes that trouble-maker's kid" each time Holly walked through her door. If I were to complain about the teacher, I would have been inclined to pull Holly out of her class. If I was going to continue sending Holly there everyday, I wanted to be on the same team. I knew I had not been able to meet all of Holly's needs on my own. So, if I could not find an alternate setting for her needs to be met, I felt that I needed to continue to work with Mrs. Turner to help her to understand and help Holly.

At the urging of a good friend, I decided to swallow my pride and call the clinic of the Communicative Disorders Department where I had graduated. I asked for an appointment to have Holly evaluated. The tone there was so welcoming. My former professors were happy to see me and Holly. They did not take the condescending, "Why don't you know?" attitude that I had feared.

I took Holly for her evaluation at the Communicative Disorders Clinic when she was almost four years old. I brought with me a cassette tape and a written transcript of a language sample in which Holly and I had talked together at home. I also brought a video tape of Holly engaging in pre-reading and playing behaviors at home. "There should be some advantages to having a client whose mother is a speech-language pathologist," I said to the clinic supervisor, Dr. Marco.

"Wow!" Dr. Marco commented. "An actual language sample in a natural setting. How wonderful!"

Dr. Marco introduced me to the graduate student, Elizabeth Harris, who would be conducting the supervised evaluation session. As Ms. Harris took Holly to one of the clinic rooms, Dr. Marco visited with me. "It's like old home week," she told me. "Another alumnus came in to have her son evaluated as well."

During the evaluation, Holly did not cooperate with Ms. Harris in her attempts to check the structures of Holly's mouth. She would not open her mouth, even for a sucker. She cried when the clinician attempted to look in her mouth and she would not imitate any sounds the clinician asked her to copy.

Holly's speech contained age-appropriate speech patterns. Examples would include saying "base" for "vase," "yewow" for "yellow," "birfday" for "birthday," "grandmover" for "grandmother," "pwate" for "plate," and "bue" for "blue." Although these productions differ from the adult pronunciations, they were acceptable because many other three and four year olds pronounce those sounds in the same way. Because of my training, I knew not to be concerned about these "errors," since children develop certain speech sounds early and others later.

During a play assessment, Holly was found to have an overall attention span of twenty minutes. It was found that Holly was able to hold her attention longer during more immature patterns of play (at a two year level) than during dramatic play. In dramatic activities, such as pretending to do something or be someone, Holly's attention span was approximately five minutes.

Ms. Harris observed that Holly appeared to be a visual learner. Holly selected toys or activities without prompting from others. Holly was not distracted by other people or activity in the room. She changed toys only when she decided she wanted to play with another toy or when given a verbal direction.

It was noted that Holly would pour beans in a cup, but did not play with the cup if there were no beans in it. Holly appeared frustrated and threw the blocks on the floor when asked to give the block to "him" (a teddy bear) or to "her" (the clinician).

Holly's pragmatic / social language was found to be at a two year level. Holly engaged in conversation with Ms. Harris and me during play activities. Her sentences contained from one to four words. However, when Ms. Harris asked her questions, Holly did not respond verbally, with gestures or with eye contact. Holly continued playing as if the question had never been asked. When Ms. Harris asked Holly yes/no questions about specific toys, Holly repeated the questions and grabbed the toys.

During the pre-literacy assessment, Holly was observed to sit in my lap to read one familiar book and two unfamiliar books. Holly looked at the pictures, did not look at other objects in the room and pointed to some of the pictures in the books. Holly imitated sentences of up to seven words in length. When reading a book, I asked, "Do you want to turn the page?"

Holly replied, "Do you want to turn the page?" as she turned it.

Ms. Harris asked Holly, "Can you put the beans in the other cup?"

Holly replied, "Can put in other cup."

Holly did not demonstrate the ability to indicate her choice from two options. Ms. Harris asked, "Is that food for me or the baby?"

Holly responded, "For me or baby."

Ms. Harris went to Holly's school to observe her in the classroom. Mrs. Turner reported to her that when she started school, Holly did not understand what was meant by the direction, "Push in your chair." Although Holly's language was improving, Holly did not use pronouns, such as "Me, mine, etc..."

The craft table was set with all the supplies needed for each student to make a Pilgrim paper bag puppet. Holly began counting the pilgrims on the table. Mrs. Turner turned to Holly to encourage her to continue counting, but Holly stopped counting, once she noticed the attention was upon her. Mrs. Turner gave the instructions for how to begin making the puppets. The other children started the activity, while Holly sat quietly and watched. Then Holly began trying to copy what the others were doing, but soon got discouraged and put the bag down. Holly did not verbally request help. Mrs. Turner noticed that she wasn't working, so she went to Holly and prompted for her to ask for help. Holly imitated her request and then Mrs. Turner began helping Holly, so that she could successfully complete the project.

It was noted that Holly did not consistently verbalize her needs. She usually engaged in whining or gesturing to elicit help. Holly did not usually initiate conversation. Holly did not use objects to create play scenes, without being an actor in that scene. For example, she did not act out scenarios with Barbie dolls or barn animals. Rather, she fed the animals or baby dolls. Her conversational speech was found to contain grammatical errors, such as, "I Mommy Tricia Kennedy is Holly's Kennedy."

Holly rarely answered questions in conversation or during reading activities. Holly had difficulty following directions requiring more than one step. She also had difficulty with differentiating between "one" and "all."

We went to a parenting workshop to teach us effective discipline techniques. They were not effective for Holly. The plan was to list privileges which would be forfeited for breaking rules. A red "X" on the chart indicated that a rule had been broken. There were three warning X's before the first privilege was lost. Holly would say, "I want a red 'X.'" We had to modify the plan and substitute a "sad face" for a "red 'X'" to get her to stop requesting them. We never did get her to see her behavior as connected to the consequences on the chart.

Dr. Marco, Clinic Supervisor, met with me during one of Holly's sessions at the clinic. "She doesn't know cause and effect," she explained. "Anything that involves 'if...then...,' she doesn't understand." I began wondering how I could ever hope to discipline a child who couldn't understand statements, such as, "If you don't pick up your toys, then you can't watch your favorite show." Dr. Marco said they would be doing basic science experiments and sequencing activities, such as making chocolate milk, to teach her the concepts of cause and effect.

"Take a little walk in my shoes," I poured my heart out to a friend over coffee at her house. "Imagine telling your three year old to do something. It's obvious that she didn't do it, but you're not sure whether or not she understood the direction. How should you respond? Is it time to explain more about what you meant or is it time to 'set firm limits?' Further, you know that she doesn't understand cause and effect and, therefore, doesn't understand consequences of behavior. If you're at school or around family, chances are the other adults will jump in and begin to tell her to stop 'being naughty' or 'act her age,' but you're still not even sure she knows what you want."

"That's a tough one," my friend empathized.

CHAPTER SEVEN

Holly seemed to think that she was in charge. When she did not like what Ken or I had said or done, she would shout at us, "Time out!" She would also try to send Shelly to time out. One morning, one year old Shelly had climbed into bed with Ken and me. Then, Holly came and climbed in the bed. Momentarily, Holly announced, "Bedtime's over; I'm going to play." I thought Shelly would want to go play too, so I lifted her from the bed to the floor so she could follow her sister. Shelly didn't want to get out of bed, so she started to cry. Holly stormed back into the room, glared at me and asked, "Did you push her?"

Holly began going to language therapy twice a week at the Communicative Disorders Clinic, in addition to attending her non-categorical preschool class three days per week. Her clinicians who worked with her directly were graduate students. They were supervised by certified speech-language pathologists, such as Dr. Marco. Her clinicians changed each semester.

Holly not only had difficulty with pronouns, such as he/him and she/her, she truly had difficulty distinguishing between boys versus girls and men versus women. If someone had long hair, they must be a girl/woman. If Shelly wore blue jeans, Holly would say, "Shelly's a boy."

For Thanksgiving, Mrs. Turner requested as many parent volunteers as possible to come and help with their Thanksgiving feast. "We will be making a complete Thanksgiving feast in the classroom." It sounded like an ambitious project since Holly was one of the oldest and most-capable students in the class.

It was interesting to watch Mrs. Turner conduct the lesson. The students were gathered around the table and Mrs. Turner would ask lots of questions, such as, "What do I need to do next?"

As the students suggested answers ("Put the beans in the pan."), Mrs. Turner would do exactly and literally as they said. Then they would laugh and modify their directions: "No! You have to open the can!" She went through numerous "mistakes," such as trying to put a metal pan in a microwave oven, and let the students correct her.

When it was time to stir, each student took a turn with the spoon. When it was time to chop, each student had the opportunity to use the knife, under direct adult hand-over-hand prompting. The kids enjoyed eating the feast they had helped to prepare.

Being in the classroom for this special occasion gave me the opportunity to meet some of the other parents. "What's Holly's classification?" One mother asked me.

It kind of reminded me of one inmate asking another, "What are you in for?"

I mumbled something about speech and language and developmental delay. I wasn't comfortable enough to ask her about her daughter's label. Later conversations I had with her made me think that perhaps it was Fetal Alcohol Syndrome.

"I know God is punishing me," she lamented with reference to her daughter's condition, "But it's not right that he's punishing her too."

"I don't consider Holly's situation to be punishing me or her," I began. "I think of it more in terms that God has a purpose for her life. He needed someone like her to be born and offer what she has to offer to the world. And He knew that we would be a family to welcome her and love her and give her that opportunity." I hoped that my words would give this mother a healthier outlook than to think that she and her daughter would go through life being punished for past sins.

"Yesterday we played with sudsy water made from dish soap," Mrs. Turner told me. "At first Holly just stood back and watched everyone else. She didn't want to put her hands in the soapy water. Then she started dipping her finger into the bubbles and wiping them on one of the other kids' hands." Similarly, on another day, they did finger painting with Kool-Aid. Holly refused to participate because she didn't want to get her hands sticky.

Potty training at school continued to be a struggle. I continued to work with Mrs. Turner and discouraged her from using punishment in the potty training. I don't think I ever won her over to my way of thinking. More and more I came to the conclusion that "If it's going to be, it's got to be me." I stopped looking at the school as "experts" in potty training and began searching for other resources to help me help Holly.

Knowing that Holly loved books and videos, I headed for the public library. I went to the children's section and checked out all the books and videos that I could find that might get Holly interested in using the potty.

I discussed with the school nurse my confusion with why Holly would wake up dry, but would refuse to use the potty during the day. "I thought bed-wetting was supposed to be the toughest problem to solve. She rarely wakes up wet. So, why do we have so much trouble during the day?" The fact was that she simply avoided toileting. Holly's attitude was "Ignore it and it will go away." It was faulty logic, but she was determined to "hold it" as long as humanly possible.

The school nurse suggested, "The first step is to put her on the toilet first thing in the morning. Don't you need to use the bathroom when you first wake up? Everyone does. So, put her on the potty when she first wakes up. That way, you'll have some success and you can reinforce the positive behavior." It sounded like good advice, but it didn't work for Holly.

She fought vehemently as I struggled to make her sit on the potty seat first thing in the morning. To ease the struggle, I started bringing the potty seat into the living room. I would take off her panties and sit her on her potty while she watched a favorite Disney Channel show. One day she argued with me, "No! Watch *Rolie Polie Olie* with my panties on!"

I related the incident to her pediatrician. "She's smart." That's all the doctor had to say about the situation.

We began watching potty videos during all our waking hours at home. Ken and I were so sick of them, we feared losing our sanity. Although Shelly was only one, she was showing more interest in the potty than Holly, due to all the books and videos in the home. I worried about how Holly's self esteem would be affected if Shelly potty trained before her. Later, I realized that Holly wouldn't have cared, because she did not compare herself to Shelly at that point in her life.

One video showed the child proudly pointing at the potty seat saying, "Mommy, look!" The video mother came in and cheered for the accomplishment.

After watching the video, Holly went to her potty seat and precisely imitated, "Mommy look!" I went to the potty seat and looked in. It was empty. Somehow, she had missed the point.

Holly needed to switch to a different animated video that included pictures of the contents of the potty seat. Without the visual cue, she didn't know what all the fuss was about.

"Do you need to go potty?" I would ask Holly at scheduled intervals or any time there were signs that she might need to.

"No," was her inevitable response.

"Are you sure?" I would ask.

"NO!!!!!!!!!!" She would scream, meaning "No, I don't want to go potty. Now, leave me alone!"

We finally began to experience some success. Holly had dry periods lasting for longer and longer times. Her accidents decreased. However, her tendency to avoid toileting continued. She would wait until she absolutely could not hold it any longer. I learned to watch for signs, such as her running around the house and whining. Then I knew that I needed to take her and force her on the toilet or she would have an accident.

The pediatrician confirmed that it was better to force her onto the toilet so that she could experience "success" than to allow her to have an accident. If she was not running around and whining on the obvious verge of an accident, we tried not to make it a power struggle. There were many mornings on which Holly went to school without having used the toilet at home.

In January of 2001, we took Holly to a local medical clinic for a health and development screening. As part of the screening, the nurse handed me a cup and directed me to take Holly into the bathroom and collect a urine specimen. "Do you have a potty seat?" I asked.

"No." She told me flatly. I couldn't believe that other parents of three and four year olds were able to get their children to pee in a cup.

I gave it my best shot. In the bathroom, I coached Holly. "This is kind of like a game," I told her. "We're going to try and get some tee-tee to go in this cup." She went ballistic. She started screaming. Everyone in the building could hear her. I'm not sure if she thought urinating in a cup violated the laws of nature or if she thought the next step might be to drink it. Whatever was going on in her mind, there was no way I was going to be able to get her to pee in that cup!

I went out and told the nurse we had been unsuccessful. She already knew. I explained more about Holly, including the fact that she was attending a non-categorical preschool class and that we had only recently begun to have success with potty training. I told her about her behaviors in avoiding toileting.

The nurse attempted to do the developmental screening, but then said that Holly was "un-testable." "I think she might be slightly autistic," she told me. I was taken aback by how casually she dropped the A-word. "That is not normal," she assessed, referring to the refusal to give a urine sample and the general toileting-avoidance behaviors.

I kept thinking, "I know she doesn't fit your definition of 'normal,' but I already told you that she is in a special education program. We realize she has some skill deficiencies, but we are working on them."

The nurse wrote a referral note to the pediatrician stating, "Please assess possible Autism. Child was un-testable. She is four and still not potty trained. Mom has to hold her on the commode to have a BM. Mom states when she needs to urinate she runs around screaming, but doesn't want to get on commode. She is in a non-categorical preschool class. Teacher states she is intelligent, but her behavior was not normal. Please assess."

I called Amanda and reported the incident to her. She discussed it with the psychologist at her work. "What does 'slightly autistic' even mean?" She asked.

"I think it's like saying 'slightly pregnant.'" He said. "I don't think there's any such thing."

The pediatrician referred us to a pediatric neurologist. Our appointment was in the spring. Holly was four and a half years old. Mrs. Turner wrote a detailed letter for us to bring to the specialist. It stated the progress Holly had made during the school year, what she could do and what difficulties she continued to have. Mrs. Turner told me she was afraid that Holly would get there and be misdiagnosed because of failure to perform to her true ability.

Mrs. Turner wrote that Holly had strengths in areas requiring rote memorization, such as recognition of letters and identifying their sounds, rote counting and identifying numbers and reading simple words. Her letter stated, "She is well behaved and generally follows the rules of the classroom. She seems to have an understanding of the basic rules of the classroom, but doesn't always seem to understand that there are consequences to the breaking of these rules." Mrs. Turner continued describing Holly as willing to play with peers, if the peers initiated the play and/or the play was directed by an adult. "She enjoys interaction with older children and adults."

Along with Mrs. Turner's letter, I wrote my own feelings about Holly's abilities and development. I wrote about what I believed were her strengths and my concerns. I listed her areas of strength as: affectionate, consistent and noticeable progress, pre-academic skills, enjoys books, enjoys interacting with peers, articulation skills, memory skills and eye contact (i.e., responds well to cue, "Look at me.").

The areas of parent concern included: following directions, failure to respond to questions, potty skills, self-help skills, gross motor skills, gender recognition, understanding expectations, jargon/echolalia, ability to ask questions, expressive communication, perseveration (ex. Asks the same question over and over until the listener is annoyed), activity level (sometimes too low, sometimes can't calm down), sensory-motor integration (ex.1, was a toe-walker when she first started walking, ex. 2, sensitive to bright light, especially sunlight, ex. 3, is bothered by clothing tags rubbing against skin), sometimes cries easily, pronouns, and social roles.

In the pediatric neurologist's office, the nurse tried to take Holly's blood pressure. It was a new experience for Holly. She became extremely uncooperative and started to cry. The nurse tried talking to her and telling her that it would be just a hug or a squeeze, but she was inconsolable.

"I don't want the blood presser!" Holly screamed. It didn't sound that great to me either when I heard her pronunciation.

After looking at the written information provided by Mrs. Turner and myself, and visiting with Holly, the doctor looked at me and asked, "So what's the problem?"

"I don't know," I stammered. "Maybe there isn't one. We just came here because we were referred."

"What's your favorite thing that your mom cooks?" She asked Holly.

"Jell-O."

The doctor laughed. "If I had seen her at the grocery store, I would have thought she was the sweetest girl I had ever met."

"Well, we think she's sweet too!" I said.

"The two big things we worry about with Autism are intelligence and communicative intent. She obviously has both of those, so I don't think there's anything to worry about. It may be that she is gifted and it's just too early to assess that."

We left that appointment feeling pleased that the doctor had been so obviously charmed by Holly, and relieved that the news had been palatable. A possible diagnosis of "gifted" was much easier to accept than "lifelong neurobiological disorder."

We went back to the nurse who had referred us. I told her the doctor said there was no sign of autism and that Holly might be gifted.

"Oh," the nurse replied. "That's great news. I'm glad you at least got it checked out. At least you know she might be gifted." I could tell she thought the doctor was nuts, but I didn't care. I wasn't feeling grateful for the referral; I was feeling irritated that she said my daughter wasn't normal!

CHAPTER EIGHT

The pediatric neurologist had recommended surrounding Holly with "normal" peers as much as possible. We checked into day care, even on a part time basis, but we couldn't afford it. Since few other opportunities existed, I started a play group one day a week at our church.

One day, we talked again about "Jesus loves you." I'm sure it was probably the millionth time she had heard that, but for some reason, it sank in at last. She left playgroup telling Grandma, "Jesus loves me, Grandma!" She kept repeating it to everyone she met.

At Mardi Gras time, we ate King Cake with the little plastic baby hidden inside. Uncle Dan, who was originally from Louisiana, had introduced this Cajun tradition when he married into the family. Holly didn't understand that whoever gets the piece of cake with the plastic baby hidden in it has to buy the next King Cake. However, she was fascinated by the little baby about the size of my pinky from top joint to tip. One day, I noticed her holding the baby and a rock in her hand. She was swaying her hand back and forth singing, "Rock-a-bye baby," or maybe "rock by baby."

I told the story to Dan and Amanda the next time they came to visit. "How come she never says any of these clever things when we're around?" Dan asked. It was as if he doubted my truthfulness in reporting the things she said. I wondered if he truly thought I was clever enough to make up all these things by myself.

My mom began to be afraid of living all alone in a big house after my dad died. First, she tried getting a dog. She bought a Cocker Spaniel mix from the Humane Society for companionship.

She named her Comet. When that wasn't enough to make her feel secure, she asked us to move out of our apartment and into a duplex with her. Believing that it would be in the best interest of everyone, we agreed.

There was some disruption in Holly's early childhood program since we had moved out of district. Eventually, we got special permission for her to continue in the early childhood class for one more year. We were told that she would definitely not be allowed to continue at that school once she started kindergarten.

"I don't know what we're going to do about kindergarten," I told my mom. "The school zone we live in now is where my friend sent her daughter and it was so rough she had to take her out and put her in the Catholic school. If Victoria couldn't handle it, I don't think it's going to be the right school for Holly."

"Well, maybe she can go to the Catholic school," Grandma said hopefully.

"Maybe, but I don't know how we'll afford the tuition."

In August of that year, my mom got the opportunity to go with some friends from church on vacation in Alaska. One of the friends had a new job as principal for a village school in Alaska. His family decided to go with him to see the sights and get him settled in before returning to Texas. They invited my mom to go with them. She was scheduled to be gone for three weeks. She left her side of the duplex and Comet in our care.

We hated to see her go, but I kept reminding four and a half year old Holly and one and a half year old Shelly that she would be back before too long. None of us predicted what was to happen next.

My mom fell in love with Alaska. She fell in love with the majestic scenery and the people she met. She learned that the village school was looking for a preschool teacher. She had always dreamed of being a teacher. For over two years she had been trying to define herself and re-design her life without my dad.

She informed us that she would be staying in Alaska to teach preschool until the school year ended. She told us we could handle the house and dog until she came home in June.

I was shocked and devastated. She was such a big part of my life; I couldn't believe that she was going to be so far away for so long. I didn't know how to begin to explain the situation to Holly and Shelly, when I didn't understand it myself.

Grandma called to talk to Holly on the phone. Holly has always had difficulty maintaining a phone conversation. She looked at the receiver and asked, "Grandma, do you live in the phone?"

After hanging up the phone, Holly said, "Grandma in Texas forever."

The next time we went to language therapy, I told them what we were going through. Holly's clinician couldn't believe it.

"Oh, no! Not Grandma!" she said, "Grandma is her whole life!"

One day, Holly found a deck of cards. She got them all out and was looking at them. She asked if the ace of clubs was an apple tree. Then she saw hearts and said, "Look! Heart! That's where Grandma is!" We had talked to Holly a lot about Jesus being in her heart. She knew that she's got a spot there for Grandma too.

"Who is my godmother?" Holly asked one day.

"Aunt Carol," I told her. "She lives in Florida."

"We're going to Florida," Holly announced at our next play group session.

"Maybe someday we can go to Florida, but we're not planning a trip anytime soon," I told her. "I'd like to go to Florida. It would be nice to see Uncle Richard and Aunt Carol."

"Yes," Holly continued. "We're going to see my godmother." I thought we must be doing something right to think Holly was so interested in her faith that she wanted to make a special trip to meet her godmother.

Later, I was enormously surprised to learn her true intentions. "We're going to Florida to see my godmother," she announced again. Then, she added, "She's going to turn me into a cat!"

I guess she didn't know the difference between regular godmothers and fairy godmothers. I called my own godmother and told her the story. I told her, "I wasn't aware that you had special powers, but now that I know, I have a few requests of my own!"

Since Holly was no longer in Mrs. Turner's class, I was surprised when she called and said she was mailing me an article. She told me, "I came across it in the waiting room of my doctor's office and the whole time I was reading it, I thought I was reading about Holly." I was instantly insulted when the article arrived and I saw the title *Why Your Child Can't Make Friends*. It was about Asperger's Syndrome.

"What does she mean she can't make friends?" I thought. "Everyone in the world is her friend!" However, when I tried to read the article more objectively, I found myself agreeing that Holly shared some characteristics with the boy featured in the article.

I discussed my concerns with Dr. Marco at the Communicative Disorders Clinic. She scheduled an appointment for us to meet with my former professor, Dr. Jones, who was widely respected in the area of language disorders. He asked me what my concerns were.

"Well, she's very intelligent, which I realize is not usually considered a problem," I began. He chuckled. "But she struggles with understanding what is expected of her in different situations and in getting along with others. She especially has trouble being still and quiet in church."

"I'd probably have trouble sitting still and being quiet if I went to your church too," he joked. "That's why most protestant churches have the kids go somewhere to play while the adults go to church."

He dismissed each of my concerns as being within the normal variation for a child of her age. He said, "If you hear hoof-beats, think horses, not zebras."

About the Autism and Asperger's he said, "If you pursue this label, you will be doing her a disservice. People will lower their expectations of her and she will never achieve her full potential."

I left thinking, "I'm not pursuing any label; I'm pursuing the truth." It wasn't that I wanted someone to tell me she had Asperger's Syndrome. It was simply that I didn't want to be failing to get her any services she might need.

Even more surprising to me was Mrs. Turner's reaction when I quoted the professor to her. "He made it sound as if I planned to take her to doctor after doctor until someone would tell me that she has Asperger's Syndrome," I reported.

She replied, "If you have to take her to doctor after doctor after doctor to get her diagnosed with Autism, then that's what you need to do because that's what's right for your child. She is too bright to get special help any other way and she will fall through the cracks without that diagnosis!"

I was still puzzled about placing her in the right kindergarten environment. I wished I could figure a way to take her to a high-priced expert experienced in assessments for things like Autism and Asperger's disorder. "I love her as much as any mother ever loved a child," I told my mom when she called from Alaska, "And some of the things she says are just precious, but there are times I still scratch my head and wonder, 'Can this be normal?'"

Professor Jones also suggested putting more emphasis on developing literacy (pre-reading and pre-writing skills). I welcomed the literacy activities, but I was sad that the next semester the student clinician had much less focus on social skills. In hind-sight, Holly has developed grade-level literacy skills. She may even be above average in reading and writing. However, she continues to struggle with social skills and peer relationships.

As a way to supplement our income, Ken and I began teaching music classes to home-school students from my mom's vacant unit of the duplex. Holly and Shelly participated in the classes. We soon learned that the home-school students exhibited much more controlled behavior than either of our girls. Shelly was only a toddler and Holly was not yet five, but it was stressful to have our children disrupt us from teaching a class for which other parents were paying us.

One parent loaned me a book that she said had been life-changing for her family. The book was based on the theme of "spare the rod and spoil the child." The author's opinions were stated forcefully. His way was the only right way, according to him. The method promoted corporal punishment using a wooden spoon. The author had no sympathy for special needs. He proclaimed that if even a dog could be taught to obey, no child was less capable than a dog.

Reading the book stirred feelings of guilt and fear within me. I wanted to do right by Holly. I wanted to teach her right from wrong and have her obey my rules. We had tried spanking her for being disobedient, but we usually found that when we used spanking as our parenting method, Holly's actions became more aggressive, rather than improving. We would observe an increase in Holly hitting us or Shelly.

"Do you have to spank your child in order to be a good parent or a good Christian parent?" I asked a friend.

"I don't think that nonsense about 'spare the rod and spoil the child' is even in the Bible," my friend said. "I think it's a myth."

"That author made it sound like I'm paving the way to Hell if I don't hit her with a wooden spoon."

"Well, he's paving the way to therapy for his kids," my friend responded.

When I got home, I took my mom's Bible Concordance on CD ROM from her desk and popped it into the computer. I scanned the digital Bible for the phrase. No exact matches were found, but it referenced the book of Proverbs, Chapter thirteen. I took out the Bible and began reading. "Here it is," I told Ken. "*Proverb 13:24: He who spares his rod hates his son, but he who loves him takes care to chastise him,*" I read.

"So what does that mean for us?" Ken asked.

"Don't you think that the point is that we're supposed to teach our kids right from wrong? The word 'discipline' means 'to teach.' I don't think that necessarily means literally that you need to beat them with a 'rod.'"

"I don't think it means that either," Ken agreed.

Still, we feared that the parents of our home-school students suspected that Holly's behavior difficulties were due to parenting "errors." We felt enormous pressure to try and increase Holly's behavior skills to an age appropriate level. Yet, we continued to feel so unsure of how to accomplish that goal.

Each night before our music class, I worried about how Holly would behave the next day. We planned a talent show for our students. Several months before, we had been in the audience at Amanda's son's talent show. Throughout the show, Holly kept calling out, "My turn! My turn!" So, for this talent show, we offered to help Holly prepare something to perform. She never seemed to understand what we were talking about in terms of choosing a song or practicing. I didn't have a clue whether she would demand to participate or refuse.

When Holly saw the others performing in the talent show, she decided she wanted a turn. She stood at the front of the room, but didn't face the audience. Instead, she watched herself in a mirror at the side of the room. She made faces and giggled at herself in the mirror. Ken and I began singing the James Ingram and Linda Ronstadt song "*Somewhere Out There*," the theme song from the movie *An American Tail,* hoping that Holly would start signing it too. Holly looked at us and said, "No!

Alleluia!" She sang the short Alleluia refrain we sing at Mass on Sunday. Some of the students giggled at her unexpected behavior. I am sure the home-school parents were wondering why we didn't either better prepare her or not have her participate at all.

When it came to disciplinary techniques, Holly just didn't seem to "get it." She seemed to have difficulty understanding expectations and / or consequences. Social rules were a mystery to her.

We attempted a new discipline plan with positive and negative consequences. We went to the store to buy some small prizes to reward the girls for consistently following house rules. Holly asked for an eight dollar Winnie the Pooh toy. We decided to let Holly and Shelly each earn points toward getting a toy of their choice as a prize. We explained to Holly that she would get the Winnie the Pooh toy, but not until she earned some points. Then we went to another department and Holly asked the sales clerk, "Do you have any points so we can get the Pooh?"

One day, I was exhausted and having "one of those days." I thought I was ready to walk out the door when I realized Shelly had gotten her clothes wet and would need a whole new outfit. (Right after I had put her socks and shoes on.) I was sitting on the floor and I was so tired and frustrated, I leaned my head on a doorknob and whined, "Oh, it's wet!"

Shelly went to another door, leaned on the doorknob and whined "Oh, it's wet!" Why are they such quick learners when it comes to bad habits?

CHAPTER NINE

Holly looked at her placemat on the table. It had a map of the United States on it. "How do we get to Texas?" she asked.

"We're in Texas," I replied, "Oh, you mean on the map. This is Texas right here."

"How do we get to Alaska?" she asked.

My heart ached a little, knowing that she was missing Grandma. I pointed, "Alaska is right here."

"That's where we go." Holly said.

"That's where Grandma lives now." I told her.

"And she's supposed to live right here in her old home." Holly pointed to Texas on the map.

On 9-11-2001, our nation was forever changed by the terrorist attacks on the World Trade Center. Holly was unaware. That happened in our world, not hers.

It did, however, affect Grandma. I'm not sure if it was the reminder that we have no guarantee of tomorrow, or what exactly made her change her mind. She decided that she was too far from home and wanted to come back.

When we got word that Grandma was coming home, we tied a yellow ribbon round the old oak tree in the back yard. We explained to Holly that the ribbon meant, "Grandma, we want you back."

Holly and Shelly went with us to the airport to pick up Grandma. After that people would ask Holly, "Did Grandma come home on the plane?"

Holly would answer insistently, "No. Grandma got OFF the plane!"

Not long after returning to Texas, Grandma went to a funeral in Oklahoma for Amanda's mother

in law. Grandma was out of town for five days.
During that time, the weather tore the ribbon off the
oak tree in the back yard. Holly was distraught. She
said, "Oh no! Grandma's ribbon! How we gonna get
it back?"

One night I went into Holly and Shelly's
room to try and get them to sleep. I read a bedtime
story and sang some lullabies. They were not calm
or quiet and no where near sleep. I told them that I
was going to leave the room since they weren't
going to sleep while I was in the room. Holly said,
"No! You're gonna make her cry! Be gentle with
your sister!" She seemed to hate to hear Shelly cry,
not so much out of empathy or compassion for her,
but simply because it was a loud, obnoxious and
offensive noise to Holly's auditory system.

There was a time when Holly would cling to
me and beg me to stay in her room at night. Then
came a time when she would run to her bed and put
her pillow over her head. She did that because she
had learned that every time I left, Shelly cried and it
was loud.

When Ken drove the car, I frequently sat in
the back seat between the two girls to "referee". It
was more difficult if I had to take them somewhere
by myself. One day, I was driving when I heard
Shelly screaming from the backseat. I looked in the
rear view mirror, but couldn't tell what was going on.
Finally, I turned around to see Holly poking her with
a straw. She was telling Shelly, "If you would hold
still, it wouldn't hurt as much." I remember thinking
that those were my words taken grossly out of
context. I had said that to Holly one day when trying
to comb the tangles out of her hair.

Another time I was trying to wash her hair in
the bath tub. Holly never liked getting her hair
washed. She said, "No! Don't touch! Just look!"

That was what I usually said when I took her with me to a store or whenever she was near breakable objects.

Holly enjoyed watching *Dora the Explorer*. At the end of each show, Dora asked, "We had so much fun today. What was your favorite part?" Holly answered, "My favorite part was swimming at my old home." After several months, she still hadn't come to terms with the fact that we had moved from our apartment. She seemed to miss the pool the most.

One weekend we went to Amanda's house in Oklahoma City. She had a cat, but it had a cut on its ear; so Amanda was keeping it in another room and didn't want it to be touched. Holly kept trying to sneak back to that room and get to the cat. I repeatedly had to chase after her and say, "No! You can't pet the cat!"

Holly yelled, "I PROMISE to pet the cat!"

"I already told her not to go back there," Amanda said.

"Yeah," I thought to myself, "I told her that too, but sometimes just telling Holly something doesn't seem to make much of a difference. Sometimes other strategies must be employed."

Grandma asked us to go with her to a Catholic church with a traditional Latin Mass. It reminded her of the church she went to as a little girl. The parishioners there were highly committed to their pursuit for holiness. Taking Holly and Shelly to Mass had always been a struggle, trying to keep them from disturbing everyone around us. They would go this way and that, as I tried to keep them pinned in and stifle their voices. Shelly was two, so onlookers could more easily excuse her behavior, but Holly was soon to be five. I could feel the judgmental stares and imagine their thoughts, "If she were my child, she wouldn't be acting like that."

There were other kids Holly's age there watching her. I imagined them thinking, "Why is she acting like that? What's wrong with her?"

In October, the fire fighter came to the public library to talk about fire prevention. "If the smoke alarm goes off at your house," he began explaining, "Run to the swing set in the backyard and wait for Mom and Dad." I looked at Holly. She was not looking in his direction and showed no outward signs of listening. It got me thinking though. Our external doors were equipped with dead bolt locks that Holly was unable to unlock. We kept the doors locked at all times. If there was a fire, Holly and Shelly would not be able to get out without adult help, but if we left the doors unlocked our little Houdini would be escaping all the time.

One day, I was folding laundry while the girls watched a show, or so I thought. I answered a knock at the door and was stunned to see the neighbor lady with Shelly. "Is this your daughter?" She asked.

"Yes," I replied taking Shelly's hand and wondering how she got out there.

"She was wandering in the street," the lady told me.

I was in shock. I had only left them for a few minutes and Shelly didn't even know how to open doors. I looked around and Holly was sitting quietly watching the TV. She must have let Shelly out and then returned to her show. I told Ken and my mom, "We have to keep these dead bolts locked at all times!" I was overwhelmed with the fear of what could have happened.

On Halloween, we went trick or treating. Grandma helped sew costumes for Holly and Shelly.

Each time the neighbors would open their door, instead of saying "trick or treat," Holly would try to walk past them and into their houses. If there was a pet inside, Holly was all the more determined to gain entry.

On a November Sunday, Holly announced that she wasn't going to go to Mass. "I'm not good in church," she said. Then she began to complain about why Comet couldn't come to church with us. Grandma became more and more annoyed with her negative, whiny attitude, especially about going to church.

"Holly, just stop that! Stop acting like that!" she scolded. It didn't seem to faze Holly.

Holly continued with her whining and fussing until Grandma decided to threaten her with time out, "Do you want to go sit in the car with Grandma?" Unfortunately, Holly interpreted it as an invitation, rather than a threat. When she seemed happy to accept the offer, my mom was even more irritated.

Because Grandma was losing patience with dealing with Holly, I sent her into the church with Shelly. I walked back to the car with Holly and told her that she was in time out. "No!" Holly shouted, "I want to sit in the car with Grandma." I tried to explain that Grandma was not happy with her and that sitting in the car would be time-out and wouldn't be fun. "Yes, it will be fun!"

We began working with our home-school students to prepare a Christmas pageant. Holly and Shelly would be in the chorus. We held auditions for the solo parts and lead roles. When it came time to sing, Holly sometimes wouldn't sing at all. Other times she proceeded to sing her own counter-melody with little concern that she was marching to the beat of her own drum. It was difficult to get Holly to enter and exit and stand in the correct place during practice. Much of the time, we tried to just carry on with the rehearsal and ignore the fact that she was wandering in and out of center stage.

During one rehearsal, the girl who was playing the role of Mary was doing her part pretending to sleep. Holly went and pretended to sleep next to her. When "Mary" got up to go on with the play, Holly told her, "Lay back down."

One day, I overheard Amanda talking with my mom. My mom was telling her that the teacher thought Holly might have some form of Autism. "Holly does not have as many special problems as you and Tricia like to think," Amanda blurted, "And, if you haven't noticed, Shelly is learning to have the same problems."

I was devastated. Someone in my family was judging me to be a poor parent. I thought it was unfair to use Shelly's behavior as proof that Holly didn't legitimately have special needs. Isn't it natural that a little sister would learn from her older sister like a role model?

Holly began hating to grow up. She started asking, "Can I be little?" "Can I be a little baby?" "Can I grow down, please?" One day she said, "...when I was a little baby and Shelly used to hold me...." She started telling everyone that she was Shelly's little sister. So, we began watching old home videos to show how big she was when Shelly was born.

One morning she watched a Barney episode about all the fun careers you can have when you grow up. I asked her, "What do you want to be when you grow up?" She didn't answer so I asked, "A doctor? A teacher? A magician? A clown?" She thought about it and answered, "A cat."

Shelly started learning to talk more. She started saying, "Let go!" when I needed to hold her down to give her medicine. She loved the telephone. She woke up from a nap one morning. She came walking into the kitchen carrying the phone with her. One day she was playing with the real phone and having quite a little conversation full of babble. She was also pushing buttons so I took the phone away from her. As I did so, she yelled into the receiver, "Bye!"

She had several toy phones which she jabbered into, then she would hand them to me for awhile and then take them back to talk some more. She was good at saying, "No," but she was also quite good at nodding, a full-body nod, complete with bending at the waist.

One day in November, Shelly began running a high fever. She was heavily congested. She lost her voice, and she complained of a sore throat.

"Holly, Shelly is very sick today." We explained.

"No," she said, "She's very, very okay." I'm not sure if it was denial or just her usual telling it like she wanted it to be.

We ended up taking Shelly to the emergency room. Although Holly only had a little congestion and an occasional cough, we decided to bring her with us. If the doctor thought Shelly was highly contagious, he might want to check Holly too. The doctor needed to take a blood sample from Shelly. Not surprisingly, Shelly cried in loud protest. Holly scolded the doctor, "Stop it!! Be nice to Shelly!" When we finally left the E.R., Holly said, "Shelly's all better now."

Of course, Shelly wasn't in fact "all better" for several more days. She still needed rest and comforting, medication and a humidifier.

"Daddy, there's a fire in there." Holly said calmly, pointing to Shelly's room. Ken looked at me with an alarmed request for clarification.

I took a peek in the room. "I guess she means the humidi-fire."

A few days later, Holly's cough got much worse. "I have a big celery cough," she told me. I wondered where that phrase came from.

One day, Holly wanted to play with Grandma's pin cushion. Grandma told her "no" and moved it to a high door chest so Holly couldn't reach. Holly got a chair, pulled it over and began to climb up to retrieve her "prize." Grandma scolded her in a firm voice, "Holly! Get down from there before you fall!" Holly burst into tears and ran for the mirror. She frequently ran to a mirror when she was crying, so she could watch herself cry.

When I went in, Holly said, "Anybody's angry." I understood that, for the first time, she realized that Grandma was angry with her. It was progress because always before Holly had not recognized the signs of anger. However, it was painful progress for Holly, and for me.

"I have a frog in my throat!" Holly said in the car as we were driving to language therapy.

"You do?" I asked.

"I have a frog in my throat!" She repeated, sounding upset.

"Holly, when people say that they have a frog in their throat, they don't mean a real frog. It's like when you have gunk in your throat and your voice sounds like this." I did my best impression of the "frog-in-throat voice." "The only way you would really have a frog in your throat would be if you ate one."

Holly was listening, quietly. She was soaking in all this new knowledge. "Some people do eat frog legs," I continued. "They say they taste just like chicken."

About that time we arrived at the clinic and I went to watch by monitor while Holly played with the student clinician. They were playing with toy food and Holly was pretending to eat a chocolate chip cookie. "What does the cookie taste like?" The clinician asked.

"Chicken," Holly replied.

CHAPTER TEN

Ken and I took the girls with us one day when we went shopping. There was something he wanted to look at in Best Buy. However, once we entered the store, Holly started running away, crawling on the floor and touching everything in sight. Shelly was copying her as fast as she could, as if the two of them had invented a great game. I told Ken, "Hurry up, get what you need and meet us at the car. We're going to time-out." I took the girls out of the store and back to the car.

When Ken got back to the car, he told Holly, "You have to be still in the store. Not running around like a chicken with your head cut off!"

Holly whimpered, "Oh no! Not cut my neck!"

On Friday mornings, when I got Holly ready to go to play group, I would tell her, "We're going to see your friends." We met as a group in the church hall. Sometimes we would plan games or activities for the kids. We had a few songs we sang each time. Then, we would have some time for free play. Problems usually occurred during the free play time. A couple of kids had a habit of talking Holly into doing something she shouldn't and then coming to me to tattle. For example, "Holly's on the table."

One day Holly came home from play group and told Grandma, "My friends laughed at me today."

One Sunday, after Mass, there was a potluck dinner in the same church hall where we usually had play group. Walking in and seeing so many people in that familiar room, Holly exclaimed, "MY FRIENDS!!!" By her inclusive definition of "friend," she had many, but I began to notice that she didn't have any close friends.

Holly was almost five when she began trying to tell jokes. Her first joke went like this. "Knock knock."

"Who's there?"

"Holly."

"Holly who?"

"Holly Kennedy." Then she laughed and laughed and laughed. I laughed too, entertained by her effort and enthusiasm.

She tried telling the joke later to Ken. He just stared at her with a puzzled look and then looked to me, as if I could explain. Holly looked at me and grinned, as if to say, "It's okay. Mommy gets my jokes."

Grandma took Holly and Shelly out in the back yard one autumn afternoon to help her in the garden. She had her back turned when Holly opened the back gate and they both ran out.

Later that evening, Ken, my mom and I talked about it. "It's almost impossible to watch them every second, but we can't afford to take our eyes off them." I lamented. "If she has the ability to open gates and doors, why can't she have the sense to know that it's dangerous?"

Holly couldn't understand death, but she would mention it sometimes. It was especially disturbing to hear her say things like, "Shelly is dead." After being told that I don't like to hear that, she said, "Shelly is dead for three minutes."

Once she told me, "I'm sorry I killed Daddy." She had interrupted him when he was playing a video game. Either the video character "died" or the "game over" was what prompted her to say that, but it was difficult to stay calm enough to talk it over rationally.

Life-threatening situations didn't scare Holly. In fact, sometimes she would say that she wanted to die and go to heaven like Papa. She said it so casually, it frightened me. It wasn't a depressed, suicidal type thought. It was like planning a destination for your next vacation. She had no comprehension of the permanence of death or heaven. She'd heard Papa was there and she thought she'd like to go visit.

I remember telling Ken, "If she starts to run out in the street, don't tell her she could die from that. She might think that's a good idea. Just keep telling her that it will hurt. She's not afraid of dying, but she doesn't like pain."

In contrast, Holly would display intense fear over situations that seemed like no big deal to the rest of us. One day she woke up with a hoarse, scratchy voice. "I lost my voice," she said, near tears. "I swallowed my voice!" She obviously believed this was a catastrophe. She ran to tell Daddy and Grandma all about it.

Holly was watching *Blue's Clues* one day. In this episode, Mr. Salt and Mrs. Pepper were having a new baby. Grandma walked into the room and Holly announced excitedly, "We're having a new baby!"

"Who's having a new baby?" Grandma asked. She was prepared to celebrate a new grandchild, not a character on a children's television program.

Later that night, I told Holly, "It's time for bed; go tell Grandma good night." She didn't want to go to bed so she refused to tell my mom goodnight. She mistakenly believed that if she didn't say goodnight, she wouldn't have to go to bed. My mom was hurt that Holly was refusing to give her a goodnight hug and kiss. She was feeling rejected, rather than seeing that Holly was essentially communicating that she didn't want to go to bed.

"Fine," Grandma said at last. "Don't kiss me good night then!" She closed her door. Recognizing that Grandma was not happy with her, Holly cried and cried.

We usually had the same problem when we were visiting and needed to go home. "Holly, say 'goodbye'," we would say, and she would begin to tantrum. I now recognize it as a problem with transitions. She was happy where she was and didn't want to leave. However, other people would get offended when she didn't go to kiss and hug them goodbye.

Holly seemed to always refuse when I said it was bath time too. She didn't want to get in the tub, but once someone forced her in, she got busy playing and didn't want to get out. She requested more water in the tub by saying, "Big, big, big water!"

One day, I had a stack of folded laundry on the dresser in our bedroom when four year old Holly walked in. She began grabbing the clothes and throwing them on the floor.

"Holly, what are you doing?"

"I'm cleaning up the room," she said. I couldn't comprehend how she could think that throwing my newly laundered clothes on the floor could be considered "cleaning."

"Stop throwing the clothes on the floor!" I demanded.

"But I have to clean up the room!"

Later, Amanda and Dan came over to visit. Holly asked her Uncle Dan, "Can I turn into a fish?"

"I guess so," he teased, "Go get me a frying pan." Holly agreed and began walking into the kitchen.

Uncle Dan called after her, "If I have a frying pan, I'm gonna cook a little fish."

Holly hugged the aquarium and said, "No! If you cook the fish, you will make them dead!" She was visibly agitated.

"Holly, he's teasing you," I explained. "Uncle Dan is not going to cook any of the fish."

Her tension ebbed away and she looked at Uncle Dan and said, "Me and the little fish are gonna eat ya!"

Holly came into the kitchen one day and asked, "Are they back?"

"Who?"

"The Williams family," she replied, referring to Uncle Richard, Aunt Carol and her cousins.

"Honey, they live in Florida. They only get to come and visit once in a long while. It's a long, long way from Texas to Florida."

"I lost my Williams family," Holly cried.

Holly's cousin called from Florida to talk to her. Holly had a lot of difficulty participating in the conversation over the phone. She slipped back into the nonsensical jargon and some of her more immature language patterns. At one point, she put the phone down beside her, on the couch. At my prompting, she picked the phone back up. I heard her cousin ask her, "You want to talk to Aunt Carol?"

Holly handed the phone to me, saying, "She said you want to talk to Aunt Carol."

Ken got some fake "Bubba Teeth" for a costume party. They look decayed. Holly and Shelly would find them around the house and want to put them in. It disturbed me to see those rotten teeth in the midst of their angelic faces. I would discourage it by saying, "Don't put those in your mouth! Those are ugly teeth!"

One day, when visiting Ken's Grandma, Holly saw her dentures floating in a bowl in the bathroom. She said, "Look at Nana's ugly teeth."

Holly's delayed language skills impacted her ability to follow verbal directions. I'm not sure when it stopped being a problem with understanding and became a habit of not following directions. As Shelly's language skills developed, her receptive language skills seemed to catch up with Holly's for awhile. We would tell Holly to do something and she would give us a blank stare. She didn't seem to have any idea what we wanted her to do. We would repeat the direction, emphasizing key words. Then repeat again and add gestures. All the while, Shelly would stare back and forth, looking at us, then Holly, then the objects involved in the direction. Finally, Shelly would complete the task we had requested of her big sister. Over time, this pattern became part of Holly's expected routine.

"Holly, take this wrapper and put it in the trash," Ken requested one day. Holly didn't budge.

"Shelly, will you put this in the trash?" Shelly happily obliged.

Later that day, I witnessed Holly telling Shelly, "Here's an orange seed. Go put it in the trash." Shelly willingly and repeatedly carried each of Holly's orange seeds to the trash can as Holly sat contentedly and ate her orange. I wondered how I was going to break the habit of Shelly being Holly's indentured servant. I was sure that Shelly would someday tire of that role.

One day, Holly came and climbed into bed with me in the morning. She cuddled close. Then she asked, "What shape are we making?"

Under the direction of the Communicative Disorders Clinic, I began making photo sequence books for Holly. The words were similar to the Social Stories introduced by Carol Gray. We had a sequence book about making cookies, a sequence book about a fishing trip we took with the Williams family one vacation, and a book about the expectations during Mass.

One morning we took the Mass Social Story photo book with us to church. We sat near the front so that Holly would easily be able to see everything that was going on. Holly didn't want to read the Mass book; she wanted to read "Holly Bakes Cookies." I told her that I didn't bring that book with me. I said she could read the cookie book at home later, but right now we were going to read the Mass book. She turned the pages of the Mass book and recited out loud the words to "Holly Bakes Cookies." I was relieved when she fell asleep for the last half of the Mass.

We watched the Disney movie *The Emperor's New Groove* in which the Emperor was poisoned and turned into a llama. The next day, Holly was choking on her Kool Aid. When I asked if she was okay, she said, "I'm turning into a llama!" Later that evening, she got out of her car seat and stumbled on my foot. With the exact inflection of the character in the movie, she complained, "You threw off my groove."

CHAPTER ELEVEN

One Friday, at playgroup, a boy came in who was Holly's age. The two of them had engaged in power struggles on previous occasions. Holly immediately changed to a confrontational tone, as soon as he walked through the door. During the play group session, they argued over toys, grabbed, hit and kicked each other. They were not forceful enough to cause real damage, but it certainly wasn't model behavior. The moms intervened and helped direct the play, and maintain the peace. Things improved, so that by the end of play group, Holly was begging to go to the boy's house to play.

During snack time at playgroup, each child had a napkin with a few animal crackers and pretzels. Holly started walking around the table eating off the other kids' napkins. When they objected, she said, "I'm just tasting."

One of the boys from play group invited us to his birthday party. As the cake was being served, Holly left her peers at the table and tried to hang out with the boy's teenage cousins. She tried to do whatever they were doing. They just kept looking at her, wondering why she didn't go back where she "belonged."

I noticed that Holly preferred playing outside by herself, when all the other kids were inside. Then Holly mixed the blue and green Play-Doh and the birthday boy started crying. He kept telling her not to mix it, so she would run and bring the Play-Doh to an adult and say, "Hold it up. Higher! Higher!"

Later, she sat in the living room, with the adults, while the kids were playing in the toy room. When another little girl came in the room, Holly's face lit up. She walked extremely close to the girl and stared at her, but didn't say anything.

"That's Annie," the girl's mother volunteered. Holly did not respond.

"And what's your name?" I prompted. Still no response.

"What's your name?" I repeated.

Holly turned around and said, "She doesn't talk."

"No," I revised. "You tell her what your name is."

"What your name is," Holly repeated.

I modeled, "My name is Holly." And she repeated it at last.

One morning after Mass, we went out for biscuits. An elderly man came to our table and said, "I want a little girl. Can I have her?" He pointed to Shelly.

I said, "No, you can't have her. She's ours. We couldn't live without her."

"Okay," he said, "Then I'll take that one." He pointed to Holly.

"No, we couldn't live without her either!"

He asked Holly, "Will you come home and live with me?"

She said, "No, I'm Mommy's baby."

"Okay," he replied, "But can I take your sister?"

Holly nodded. The man laughed and walked away. Ken and I quickly began trying to explain that the man was teasing, but that he was a stranger and you never leave with a stranger. We told her that we didn't know him, and you can't tell which strangers are good and which strangers are bad. We told her that it is not safe to go with a stranger. We told her it is dangerous.

Holly kept saying things like, "But he was happy." And "It is safe to go with strangers; the stranger liked me."

94

For weeks, Holly would point and say, "There's a stranger in that car. The stranger is okay. There's another stranger."

One summer day, Holly and Shelly went to a park. A lady I worked with was there with her son. Shelly and the boy started playing while I talked with his mom. A few minutes later, I heard an irritated voice. I turned to see what the kids were up to.

"Stop throwing those tomatoes!" A lady scolded. Her house was adjacent to the park and her tomato vines wove in and out of the chain link fence surrounding her yard. "Those tomatoes are for eating; not for throwing!"

"But I don't eat tomatoes," Holly defended.

"Well, I do!" the lady asserted, her voice growing louder with disapproval. "They're my tomatoes and I like to eat them and I don't want them thrown on the ground and wasted!"

Holly and Shelly and the boy began walking towards us with their heads down in shame. "Sorry, guys," I heard Holly say. "I got us in trouble! I made up a bad game!"

Just before her fifth birthday, Holly began noticing writing everywhere. She would name the letters on street signs, cereal boxes and t-shirts and ask, "What it says?"

Holly sometimes cried easily. Around age five, she began crying any time someone used a harsh voice with her. One night, Grandma showed Holly her pretty breakable Christmas decorations. Later, she saw Holly playing with them. She said, "No, no, no! Those are just for looking; they aren't for touching!" Holly burst into tears. My mom looked at me and asked, "Is she tired or has she just forgotten that Grandma scolds her sometimes?" A little later she scolded her for something else and

Holly started crying. "Fine," Grandma said, "Just be a little crybaby then."

In my mind, I was thinking, "No name-calling." Still, I wondered how my mom could have so much difficulty dealing with Holly, at times like these, in spite of all her experience with other children. What made Holly different?

Holly frequently complained about loud noises. She would also hit her ears with her hands. She would do that when someone was scolding her.

One day, Amanda was scolding Holly. Holly held up her hand as if to say, "stop." Holly was upset about Amanda's angry voice. Amanda was upset because she interpreted the gesture to mean, "Talk to the hands 'cause the ears aren't listening."

Later, Grandma gave each of the girls a piece of cake. Shelly proceeded to get hers all over herself and then crawl under the table with the dog. I looked at her and said, "Shelly, you're a mess!"

Holly said nonchalantly, "Comet is cleaning her up."

Holly began asking, "Where is my brother?" We told her that she didn't have a brother, only a sister. "But I need a brother." One day at church, she pointed to a tall teenage boy in the pew behind us. "I want a brother like that!" she said.

"The only way you will ever have a brother," I began explaining, "is if God sends a baby boy and puts him in my tummy." Holly reached into my shirt.

"I'll get it," she said.

A few days later, we went to the store. Ken pushed Holly and Shelly in the cart, as I hustled around trying to get what we needed, so we could get out of there. Holly called, "Mommy, you're getting too far away from your family!"

Richard and Carol came to visit and brought a friend. Richard and Carol stayed in my mom's part of the duplex. We talked to Holly about staying in our room so that Richard's friend could borrow her bed. She said, "But I want to sleep with him." When he arrived, she greeted him by saying, "I want to sleep with you."

By age five, Holly began to recognize and tell people, "You're teasing me."

I visited Holly at Mrs. Turner's class. Mrs. Turner asked her, "Holly, what did we do today?"

Holly said, "We had fun."

"Yes," Mrs. Turner said, "But what did we do over here in the Christmas Corner?"

"We decorated the tree."

"Yes. And what did we do after that?"

"We looked at it."

Mrs. Turner laughed. "And what did we do after that?"

Holly laughed. "We looked at it some more."

One evening, I was trying to relax Holly, by gently scratching her back at bedtime. She told me, "Stop raking me!"

I said, "Oh, I'm sorry. I thought you would like that. I was just scratching your back."

"It's not nice to scratch people," she said.

Prior to age five, Holly had no qualms about eating or drinking after anyone else. The more she learned about germs, the more particular she became. It was not an abrupt and total change. At first, she would only drink after someone if it was soda, or something she desperately wanted. Then she began to refuse to eat the rest of an ice cream cone if I had licked one of the drips. She became adamant and vocal about not eating or drinking anything that had been "contaminated" by Shelly's germs.

One day, we were each having a glass of ice water. Her glass was soon empty, so I poured the rest of mine into her glass. Holly said, "Now that's yours."

One night at the dinner table, Holly kept saying, "This is yucky! Yucky! Yucky!" Ken and I told her that it was rude to insult a chef's cooking like that. She was not using good table manners. We warned her to stop saying it, or she would have to go to time out. "But it's yucky!" she kept protesting repeatedly. We put her in time-out and she cried and cried, like she couldn't see it coming.

A couple days later, I saw her put her baby doll in the microwave of her toy kitchen and say, "You're in time-out."

I asked, "What did the baby do?"

Holly explained, "She said 'yucky.'"

"Look, Holly," I said one day. "There's a bird's nest in that tree."

"Mama bird laying eggs in the nest," she replied.

"I don't know if there are any eggs in there right now. It's winter, but maybe in the springtime."

"Please!" she pleaded.

"Holly, I don't have any control over that. I can't make the mama bird lay an egg!"

"Please! Please! Please!" she continued to beg. I've never liked it when she begged after I told her no, but it seemed utterly absurd for her to be begging for something so completely out of my control.

For lunch, Holly said she wanted raw eggs. I explained to Ken that she meant boiled eggs. He boiled eggs and prepared an egg salad. She looked at her serving and said, "I don't want scrambled eggs; I want raw eggs." She was upset that they were not one solid egg shape.

One night, I got cold, so I slipped on a pair of warm-up pants. Holly recognized them as pants I sometimes wore over my swimsuit, on the way to the pool. She asked, "Why are you wearing swimming pants?"

Grandma gave Holly a cookie. Holly took it, said nothing, and started walking away. My mom prompted her by saying, "Thank you."

Holly turned around and said, "You're welcome." Holly told me, "Grandma gave me a cookie."

"Did you say 'thank you?'" I asked.

"No, Grandma did," she replied. "Can I have the 'nother cookie?" She asked meaning "another."

Holly told Ken, "Daddy, when you turn into Santa, you can bring me a hamster." She remembered seeing him dress up in a Santa costume the year before.

We bought her a hamster for her fifth birthday. She named it "Buddy." We thought it would help her to learn responsibility. We were wrong. One day, she was holding the hamster. She was always excited around it which made her loud and hyper. She squeezed it too tight and it bit her, breaking the skin.

"Ow!" She wailed. "Buddy gave me a shot!"

Another day she was holding Buddy, but she let him get away from her. Buddy scrambled across the floor and Comet caught him in her mouth in an instant. Immediately, I pried the hamster out of Comet's mouth, but the damage was done. Buddy died. It was sad, and traumatic. Holly talked about it incessantly.

We bought Holly a miniature hamster, to ease the loss of the original. Holly named the new hamster Buddy too. Then she would talk about "Big Buddy" and "Little Buddy."

My mom had dried some roses from a bouquet. Holly and Shelly got hold of them and pulled all the petals off. When Holly saw Grandma coming, she ran and hid.

My mom told her, "You knew you weren't supposed to be doing that, or you wouldn't have ran and hid." The problem was she did it impulsively, without thinking through the consequences. She realized it was a mistake in hindsight, when she saw Grandma coming.

Holly started crying and ran and threw her arms around me. I felt torn. I wanted to comfort my child, who was quite upset, but I didn't want to contradict my mom, who was trying to teach her to respect other people's property. I told Holly to tell Grandma she was sorry. She wouldn't. That was not any easy word for her. To apologize, you need to be able to understand the situation from the other person's point of view. Holly could not. I carried her over to Grandma and said, "You need to hug and make up with Grandma."

They hugged, but then my mom said, "I give hugs very freely, but I tell it like it is." I was frustrated, because it seemed like she was scolding Holly again. I prefer action, consequence, resolution. At some point, I think Holly needed the reassurance that we still love her, and are not holding any grudges against her.

Holly said, "We have to get Grandma a new rose. Then she will be happy."

Holly walked into my room carrying a pair of my mom's socks. I told her to take them back to Grandma. "I'm just taking care of them," she said.

One day, Holly saw some pots of dead flowers outside the church. She said, "Oh. The flowers are dead. Don't worry, Flowers; you'll be alive soon."

Holly said, "I miss Jesus."

"You don't have to miss Jesus, because he's always with you. He's in your heart." I told her.

"Jesus is going to die again," she said.

"No," I explained. "Jesus is alive forevermore. He died one time to win over death. He died one time to save us so we can all live in heaven one day."

"Yes," she said, "I'm gonna go to heaven."

"She talks about heaven the same way she talks about Florida or Alaska," I thought.

My mom bought a new desk. Holly hid under it and behind it. She said, "Grandma, I like it. I like the hiding places."

I heard Holly and Shelly arguing in the other room. Holly ran to me saying, "Mommy, she's gonna spank me!"

"Who?" I asked.

"Shelly!"

Later, Holly was lying on her back in the bath water letting her hands and feet float to the surface. She asked, "Why are my feet up? Why are my fingers up?"

As a five year old, whenever Holly saw someone sleeping, she felt compelled to wake them up. She would wake Shelly, Ken or me, if we were napping. The result was always that she was greeted by extremely grumpy people. Holly would simply say, "Wake up; it's morning!"

Holly pushed a chair over to the refrigerator, stood on it, and tried to get the flashlight from up top. "I can't reach," she said.

"You're not supposed to be able to reach," I told her. "That stuff is up there so you won't get it."

"Don't worry," she replied. "I'll get it."

"No," I corrected. "You're not supposed to get it."

"Don't worry; you'll get it," she tried.

I said "No" and removed her from the chair, despite her protests.

Grandma has a hearing impairment. We were trying to watch a Christmas movie as a family. It was difficult to find a volume that was loud enough for Grandma to hear, without being too loud for Holly to tolerate. We tried putting cotton in Holly's ears, but that didn't work because she was sensitive about having anything in or touching her ears.

We decorated our Christmas tree. Holly was five and Shelly was two. Although they both enjoyed decorating the tree, Holly kept getting increasingly frustrated with Shelly because Shelly liked to remove the ornaments from the tree.

Things that don't matter to most people sometimes matter to Holly. She stopped wanting to use her *Blues Clues* toothbrush because the handle was too wide to fit in the toothbrush holder. I opened a new adult toothbrush and she brushed her teeth. When I put the toothbrush away, she corrected me and pointed to a different hole of the holder that it "needed" to be in.

"Who's in our heart?" Holly asked.

"You're always in my heart because I love you." I answered.

"You're in my heart because I love you too," she said.

"And Jesus is in our hearts too." I added.

"Jesus is in my heart three." Holly said.

CHAPTER TWELVE

In the spring, Holly had the opportunity to attend a regular pre-kindergarten class, in addition to the special education early childhood class. We were thrilled that she would have the opportunity to interact with "normal" kids her own age.

One day, I received a note from the pre-K teacher, Mrs. Lopez, saying that Holly had scratched a peer when the peer took the hat off Holly's head. My guess is that Holly probably dug her nails into the other child's arm. I'm basing my guess on my observations of how Holly treated Shelly when such disputes arose.

I told Holly that she needed to write an "I'm sorry" card. I wrote the words, reading them aloud as I wrote, "I'm sorry I hurt you. Please forgive me and be my friend. OK?"

Holly corrected me saying that I should not have written "I hurt you," but "I scratched you." She either did not understand or refused to admit that she hurt the girl when she scratched her. I told her she needed to color some pictures on the card. She said, "I'm going to draw a witch."

"In order to apologize," Dr. Marco later explained, "She has to have reciprocal emotion. She has to understand how the other person is feeling. Otherwise, it just becomes a habit that you say 'sorry' whenever you're in trouble. We used to have a student who would hit us just so he could say 'sorry.' That was some fine teaching that we did there!"

In March, we began to get serious about kindergarten plans for the next school year. We determined that we would not be satisfied to send her to the school for which the duplex was zoned. The most obvious choices we could see were private school, home-school or Spanish Immersion at the school where Holly had attended Mrs. Turner's class.

The elementary where she went to Mrs. Turner's class was a good school in a good area. However, Holly wasn't eligible to go there as a regular kindergarten student, since we no longer lived in that district. She would have been eligible to attend the Spanish Immersion program, since most schools didn't have such programs.

"I don't know if she could handle learning a second language. She's having some trouble learning her first one," I commented. I did some research about learning a second language with a language disorder. The research seemed to suggest that a student with a language disorder would be equally able to learn a second language as their first language. The research did not believe there was harm in exposing a child to a second language.

"She is so bright," I considered. "Regular kindergarten might be boring for her. If everything were in Spanish, it would certainly make it more challenging." Still, I wasn't sure about the idea.

The deadline came to register for Spanish Immersion. I decided to go fill out the paper work, to keep our options open. I was in the office, discussing my concerns about Holly's language disorder. Meanwhile, Holly was next to me, jumping up and down, making loud giggly noises and flapping her arms. Once, she ran out of the room and down the hall, and I had to go retrieve her. Several other times, I had to physically restrain her from running away. I thought, "I'm sure these people are excited about the prospect of having her in their program."

Then, when we were ready to leave, she whined and ran away from me and threw herself on a couch in the lobby. She didn't want to leave without playing with all the children that she had imagined would be there. My explanations that there are no children at the school board office did not convince her. I just had to carry her to the car.

I had the opportunity to observe Holly in her regular pre-Kindergarten class on two separate mornings before making a final decision about a second language. After seeing her in a general education English-speaking class, I decided to "just say no" to the Spanish Immersion program. I realized that I routinely observed her in one on one or small group interactions. She excelled in those settings. I was surprised to see, that in a class of approximately eighteen students, she rarely volunteered to answer, even when I knew that she knew the answer.

For example, she had known how to identify all the letters of the alphabet for over a year. She was beginning to sound out words and read simple books. She could read all the days of the week on the calendar, and in other contexts. Her teacher pointed to the "W" in "Wednesday" and asked, "What letter does this start with?" Holly did not raise her hand, or give any indication that she knew the answer. Her teacher probably underestimated her abilities, because Holly was not demonstrating what she knew or what she could do.

The few times Holly attempted to participate, she was ignored because she was inappropriately answering without raising her hand. I think if Holly's teachers and peers were speaking Spanish, she might have given up on participating. She may have begun to treat her entire school day as if it were white noise (static).

Realizing that Holly was not a good candidate for a foreign language immersion program was a little disappointing for two reasons. First, it's tough to accept our children's limitations. Second, I had to accept that Holly would not be able to continue going to the same school the next year. Spanish Immersion students are allowed to go out of zone, but not Holly.

We placed Holly on the waiting list to attend kindergarten at our local Catholic school. We met with the principal and discussed Holly's strengths and weaknesses. We reported that she had already attended a special education preschool setting. The principal said that he could not agree to take Holly as a student, unless the kindergarten teacher was sitting next to him saying that she could handle it. He said we would discuss it further if a kindergarten slot became available.

I was shocked to learn that we not only had to worry about three thousand dollars per year tuition, but that they might not accept her, even if we had the money. Mrs. Turner told us that Holly had already mastered most of the Texas academic benchmarks for kindergarten. However, she was not sure whether or not a private school could meet her needs. She asked again whether or not we had taken her to a doctor to determine if she had Asperger's Syndrome.

"You may not think she has an advanced vocabulary, since she qualifies as language impaired," Mrs. Turner began. "She doesn't often make use of her vocabulary. However, at times, she says words that the average child her age would not use."

Mrs. Turner continued to be concerned about Holly's social skills. She told me that one afternoon a little girl had wanted to play house and pretend to be Holly's mom. Holly said, "No. My mommy's coming to pick me up." The teachers tried to explain that it was pretend, but Holly refused to play and sat down and pouted.

Mrs. Turner reported that Holly continued to have trouble reading other people's body language and facial expressions.

On our way to language therapy, Holly said loudly, "It's all right to say 'hi' to strangers."

"As long as you're with me, it's all right to say 'hi,' but you have to stay with me and you never leave with a stranger," I re-emphasized.

Holly kept saying "Hi!" to all the college guys we passed on campus. They ignored her and kept walking. They were all involved with their own conversations. "They're not saying 'hi' to me!" Holly complained.

"That's their choice." I explained. "We're strangers to them, and they don't feel like talking to strangers."

Holly said "Hi" to a young male African-American student. He returned her greeting and Holly loudly announced, "That brown boy said 'hi' to me!"

We walked by a guy sitting on a brick wall surrounding a pond. Holly said, "Look at this boy." I assured her that I saw him and tried to hurry her along. She said, "He's doing a bad, bad job today."

In the clinic waiting room, Holly went up to a teenage client who was minding her own business. Holly handed her a magazine saying, "You're a girl. Here you go." Then she stood in front of the girl's mother and asked, "Are you a girl or a boy?"

Her student clinician gave Holly an Easter basket. The basket was filled with plastic eggs and each egg contained chocolate candies. I could tell her clinician was disappointed because Holly seemed to take it for granted.

"Holly, you're supposed to be excited." She said.

"She's excited; just in her own way," I assured the student clinician. I kept thinking, "If you want to know how much she cares about it, try telling her she can't take it home." She would have thrown a fit! I had to cue Holly with the appropriate response, "Tell Ms. Young 'Thank you.' Give her a hug. Wish her a happy Easter." Holly followed each direction robotically, but her student clinician did not seem to believe that Holly was genuinely appreciative of the gift.

Holly has an excellent memory. Sometimes we were startled by things she remembered. One day, she met a distant cousin, for the first time. She kept calling her, "Girl! Girl!" or referring to her as "that girl."

I told her "That girl's name is Casey."

Holly laughed and said, "Uh! Casey is a boy dog's name!"

I looked at Ken and asked, "Who do we know that has a boy dog named Casey?" It sounded familiar, but I couldn't remember.

Ken said, "Kayla and Roy." They were friends of ours who had moved to Houston about a year earlier. It had been about two years since Holly had seen their dog and she had only seen it once.

One day we went to Subway for lunch. Holly walked up to a table with three young men in their 20's or early 30's. They were all wearing matching orange shirts. The shirts said, "Cox Cable," but Holly couldn't read or understand that. I noticed that the shirts were the same color as the prison workers you can see along the highway, but, of course, Holly didn't know that either. She told the men, "My name is Holly Kennedy and my phone number is 2-3-7-8-2-6-2."

I told her, "You're not supposed to tell that to strangers."

Later, she said, "When I grow up, I'm going to be a stranger like them." She pointed to the table of young men.

One day, I asked Holly if she knew that school was going to be closed. She told me she did know because we were going to celebrate "Dr. Martin Luferking." She told me that she had learned all about "Dr. Martin Luferking" at school.

I told Mrs. Turner that I was unsure about whether or not Holly met the definition of Asperger's Syndrome. Unfortunately, in many ways it seemed that she was "too impaired" to have Asperger's. For example, the things I was reading stated that children with Asperger's had average to above average language development and Holly had an identified language disorder. Kids with Asperger's were said to have normal self-help skills and Holly was delayed.

"But her topics of obsession!" Mrs. Turner exclaimed.

"I didn't think she had any topics of obsession," I said, surprised. "What are her topics of obsession?"

"Jesus, baby brother and Buddy, the hamster."

I had never thought of those things as "topics of obsession." When Holly talked about God and Jesus, I thought that meant we were doing a good job as parents. We were teaching her to put God first and love Jesus.

"But she comes up with these facts that a child her age would not normally know!" Mrs. Turner commented. Holly had questions; we had answers.

I never thought of the baby brother or hamster as topics of obsession either. I thought that she wanted a brother. She would say, "I already have a sister." I also considered it normal for a child to talk frequently about her pet.

In response to Mrs. Turner's urging, we scheduled an appointment with a child psychologist in April to try and settle the issue: does she have Asperger's Syndrome or not? In the psychologist's office, we talked about Holly's exaggerated reactions to pain. The psychologist encouraged me to keep a pain journal and write what happened and what the response was.

When Holly fell and scraped her knee on the sidewalk, she screamed and cried and talked about dying. She didn't want anyone to touch it. Even hours later, she didn't want to get in the bath water. She didn't want anyone to touch it the next day and she continued talking about dying. My response was to try and calm her down. I kept assuring her it was just a scrape, and she wasn't going to die. The most effective way to distract her was to sing to her.

Little Buddy bit her, but did not break the skin. She screamed loudly for ten minutes and cried real tears. I rocked her and talked to her to calm her down.

A few days later, she started making gagging sounds and slapping her stomach. I had no idea what the problem was. I kept prompting her with "Use your words," but she would only mouth nonsense. I was bewildered. At first, I thought she was going to throw up. Eventually, about half an hour later, I figured out that she had the hiccups. Then, I relaxed about it and just reassured her that she was going to be all right.

Later that same day, she was walking barefoot on dry grass. She screamed "Ow!" as if needles were piercing her feet. I helped her back to the sidewalk.

Holly never liked to have stickers on her. Likewise, she did not like to put band-aids on. If she needed a band-aid, she would cry and jerk away. Someone would have to physically hold her down to put the band-aid on.

At our next appointment with the psychologist, an interview format was used to complete the *Childhood Autism Rating Scale (CARS)*. Ken and I were seated next to each other, answering each question. Ken was still not entirely comfortable with the idea of having Holly evaluated. He was not prepared for the results of the evaluation. I was aware that he wanted to be told that she was "normal," so I was cautious in my responses. If I was "very concerned" about an interview item, I would only admit to being "somewhat concerned."

When all was said and done, Holly's score was 29.5. The psychologist said she would have needed to achieve a score of 30 to be considered "Mildly Autistic." He said that we had insufficient evidence to suggest that she was Autistic. He told us, "I wouldn't be too worried. She may be in her own world, but she allows visitors."

When I mentioned some of our struggles with trying to help Holly understand behaviors and consequences, he said, "So, you have a difficult-to-love child. So do I."

I could not have been more shocked if he had reached across the room and slapped me in the face. I wanted to say, "I don't know your child, but my child is not difficult to love. Holly might be difficult to discipline, but she is certainly not difficult to love!"

The psychologist's summary report stated, "By parent description, she almost seems to have characteristics of Asperger's Syndrome. However, she did not present as a child with Asperger's Syndrome in this office." I was annoyed with the process and the result. I felt that, once again, the so-called "expert" understood less about Holly than I did.

The Shrine Circus came to town. Holly and Shelly got to ride an elephant. We had to skip riding the camels, miniature horses and fun jump because of a lack of funds. We enjoyed the show: elephants, high wire, tigers, etc... Holly thought she'd like to grow up and do all of that stuff. I rather hoped she wouldn't. She was watching the tight rope walkers and thinking she'd like to try. I was remembering that sometimes she trips over her own feet just walking on the floor.

One day Holly asked, "What is Jesus' name?" I wasn't sure what she meant. Then I decided maybe she was curious about his last name.

For lack of a better response, I said, "His name is Jesus Christ."

She looked at me funny, and then said, "Jesus' name is 'Amen.'" Then I remembered our children's prayer book, in which every prayer ends with "In Jesus' name, Amen.'"

For dessert I offered her a piece of chocolate cake with coconut icing. She pointed to the icing and asked, "What's that?"

I said, "It's called German Chocolate cake."

"Yuck! Germs!" She protested. Despite my explanations that "GERMAN" had nothing to do with "germs," she chose not to eat the cake.

One morning in May, Holly cried and said she swallowed a frog. I told her it wasn't a real frog and wouldn't hurt her. She said it was real. She whined at breakfast. At school, she told Mrs. Turner she wanted Mommy. Since I had not yet left the school, she walked to me. When she got to me, she threw up. I had no idea she was feeling sick. She never said anything about her tummy bothering her.

The next day she stubbed her toe. She screamed and fell on the floor and cried for five minutes. Ken told her, "You're okay."

Holly said, "No. Mommy needs to talk to me."

CHAPTER THIRTEEN

Near the end of Holly's pre-kindergarten school year, Ken flew to Michigan for an interview for the Music Minister position at a Catholic Church in Mid-Michigan. He hadn't even had time to unpack when he got back home before Father Ben called and offered him the position.

We were unsure about how we could help Holly through such a major transition. When we moved from our apartment to the duplex with Grandma, Holly talked continually about going back to "our old home." She didn't believe that the duplex was her home. What would she think about moving again? How would she adjust to moving so far away? How would she handle being away from extended family?

We began talking to Holly about the idea of moving, trying to get her started preparing for another transition. Ken had sent resumes to various music-related job openings. At first, we were not sure which job offer would come through, so we talked about the different places we might move. We told her that we were not sure yet where God wanted us to go. It would be a big surprise.

One day Holly said, "We're going to move to 'Sarf Carlina.' My Godmother and Godfather are going to move there and we'll all live in a big house in 'Sarf Carlina.'"

I had promised to follow Ken to the ends of the earth, if that's what it took for him to get a job that would allow him to support the family. So, once the job offer was confirmed, we were on our way to Michigan.

I talked to one of my speech colleagues about our concerns for Holly's development and education. She said, "Maybe there's a reason beyond Ken's job that you're going to Michigan."

It wasn't long before Ken was having a telephone conversation with Father Ben, his new boss, about our plans for Holly's kindergarten. Father Ben wanted us to enroll Holly in the Catholic School for the parish. "You need to explain to him that she has special needs and needs to be in a public school for the support services," I told Ken.

I remembered my experience with the Catholic School principal in Texas. At that point, I felt like Catholic schools not only couldn't meet her needs, but didn't even want to try.

In contrast, Father Ben was giving Ken his best sales pitch. He assured that the public school system in his area sent support staff to the Catholic school to work with students who qualify. He felt strongly that they could meet Holly's needs. So, we began to consider the Catholic school as our first option for Holly's kindergarten.

One of our biggest sales pitches to Holly, regarding the move, was that we would be moving to an apartment with an indoor swimming pool. We found the apartment online and made arrangements to move-in, sight unseen. We drove a moving truck for two entire days, with an over-night stay at a hotel, to get to our new home. When we arrived, Holly was more than ready to jump into the long-anticipated swimming pool. We went right away to the pool and found out it had closed for the night, about half an hour earlier. Holly had a major meltdown, crying inconsolably right there in front of the rental office of our new apartment complex. I could only imagine what all our new neighbors thought of her and us.

The next day we made sure to go to the pool early. We got our swim suits on and walked to the rental office. We noticed the overcast skies, but we thought, "Who cares? It's an indoor pool." When we arrived at the office there was a sign that said, "Pool closed."

Holly started melting down again, screaming and crying, "No! The pool is not closed! The pool is open! We have to go swimming!" Ken went in to ask why the pool was closed.

"Because of the weather," he was told.

"But it's an indoor pool," he complained.

"But if lightning struck the building, the pool is the first place it would go."

"But there's not even any lightning! There's just a little distant thunder."

"Well, thunder is lightning."

Unable to change the circumstances, I scooped our screaming, crying, broken-hearted Holly into my arms and carried her back to our apartment. People stared, as if we must be exceptionally poor parents to "allow" her to throw such a fit. Ken and Shelly drooped along behind. After those two incidents, we learned that we could not tell Holly that we would go swimming. We had to develop a new rule of saying, "Let's go walk over and see if the pool is open." Experience was teaching us these lessons the hard way.

One day, the pool was open and we got to swim. The girls were having a grand time. Holly was jumping from the side into the 5 foot deep mid-section of the pool. In the shallow end, she would jump up and down, plunging under the water and springing back up again. She seemed as if she could be happy there forever. Then, a boy vomited in the pool, and the management had to clear everyone out, so they could shock the pool. Holly could not understand. She melted down again and I carried her home once more.

It was quite upsetting when life did not proceed according to Holly's expectations. Sometimes, we unwittingly contributed to the wrong expectations. For example, before we moved, we told Holly that we were moving to Michigan, and it is shaped like a mitten. She seemed to like that idea. I became concerned when I heard her tell someone, "Our new house is shaped like a mitten." We had to show her the map and emphasize that the state is shaped like a mitten, not our new apartment.

The transition from Texas to Michigan was difficult for the kids, in ways we had not foreseen. We had difficulty convincing Shelly and Holly that they should to go to sleep before ten o'clock at night, even though the sun was still up. Holly said, "In Texas it gets dark before bedtime." However, she loved the Michigan ants because they were not fire ants, like in Texas. One day, she was looking at a group of ants and said, "Which one do I choose?" Then she picked one up and carried it around. I began to wonder if she would grow up to be a scientist. One day, at McDonalds, she was totally unaware of the other kids playing, as she studied a lady bug she had found.

The time came for Ken's first weekend as Music Minister in our new church. He played the organ, and directed the Sunday choir. I especially missed having anyone with me to help with the girls.

Since we only had one car, we had to arrive with Ken at least half an hour early. On top of that, the Masses were longer than what the girls were used to. It was a real challenge, just to try to keep them from disrupting the entire congregation. I was constantly concerned that Holly and Shelly's behavior, and my inability to control their behavior, would reflect poorly on Ken in his work environment.

I was thankful that the alleluia was up-beat and included snapping. The choir was tickled by Shelly, because she was dancing along, and bouncing her hand and arm in rhythm, even though she didn't know how to snap.

The children got to bring up their offerings (monetary and a statement of their good deed for the week) and put them in Father's basket at the front of the church. They also held hands during the Lord's Prayer, greeted each other before Mass, sign of peace and coffee and juice after Mass. It was very welcoming and family-oriented.

I looked around at the other kids in the church. Most were sitting quietly, throughout the Mass. Holly and Shelly had moments in which they participated wholeheartedly (ex. during some of the singing and the sign of peace). At other times they might be seen wiggling around, lying down, talking, etc...

I knew that some people probably thought it would have been better if I kept them home "until they learned how to behave," but I believed they were getting something out of the Mass.

One of the choir members walked into the church and Holly said, "Look, its Aunt Carol." I think she just missed family enough that anyone who looked vaguely similar could be confused.

Shelly said, "It's not Aunt Carol. Just a copy." Since I was also missing family, I decided that there's nothing like the original!

The first Sunday, we had two Baptisms during Mass. The church had a big Baptismal font near the entrance. The next Sunday, Shelly saw a baby and said, "Baby wants to take a bath." I decided she must have thought we ought to dunk one every week.

Holly brought her stuffed Pooh bear with her to Mass. Each time anyone asked her name, she added, "This is Pooh. He's a willy, nilly, silly old bear."

The next Sunday, Holly woke to realize she had lost her voice. Each time that happened, she would freak out. Then when it returned, she would be ecstatic. I don't think she accepted it as just something that happens when you get sick. For her, it seemed more like when the Sea Witch stole Ariel's voice on *The Little Mermaid*.

She was exceptionally good that Sunday, during the first part of Mass, but I think it was because she didn't feel well. Her energy must have come back around the middle of Mass, because she started picking on Shelly. Then they were both a handful until the recessional hymn ended.

I was exhausted by the time we got home. After lunch, I went to bed and slept until almost five o'clock in the evening! I couldn't believe it when I saw the clock. I still felt like I needed more sleep.

With Mrs. Turner's cautions and promptings about not letting Holly fall through the cracks, we began to research where we could take Holly for a comprehensive evaluation and diagnosis. In Holly's preschool setting, teachers had been strictly told not to mention the word "Autism" to a parent, unless the child had already received that medical diagnosis by a physician. "She's too bright to receive services under any other classification," Mrs. Turner had insisted. "That's why it's imperative that you take her to get a medical diagnosis."

We found two or three places that seemed to specialize in diagnosing Autism Spectrum Disorders. However, they quoted an average cost of approximately three thousand dollars. I didn't even have to call for a bank balance to know that we couldn't afford that. Instead, I called our health insurance company. After being transferred around from department to department, I was more discouraged than ever.

The insurance company's position in a nutshell was: "We'll have to have our doctors make a determination about whether this is a health issue or a mental health issue. If it is a mental health issue, you could see a psychologist, but then you only have 50% benefits. If it is determined to be a physical issue, then you will receive 80% benefits, but you will not be able to see anyone, other than a medical doctor."

"It doesn't take a rocket scientist to figure out that the head is connected to the body!" Ken complained. I agreed.

It helped when I met a couple of other parents who had children on the Autism spectrum. "If I were you," one mom told me, "I wouldn't bother with trying to get a medical diagnosis. The school is going to insist on doing their own evaluation anyway."

"Really?" I was surprised. It seemed the opposite scenario from the way the education system operated in our previous location.

"What you need to do," she continued, "is request a special ed. evaluation. Be sure to request evaluations from the School Psychologist, Social Worker and Speech Pathologist, because those are the ones who are required to determine if someone qualifies under the ASD classification." How would I have ever known to do that without this helpful mom?

"It would be great if you could get the opinion of the Autism Consultant, but there are two problems with that."

"What are the problems?" I asked.

"Well, we happen to be between consultants in our district right now. Plus, the schools don't like to let the consultants get involved until after the initial evaluation has determined that the child qualifies as ASD."

"Oh," I said, trying to process all of that information.

"You could call the district you live in and see if their autism consultant could come and observe Holly in her classroom. It would be worth a shot." I thanked her for all of her help and made note of all of her suggestions.

In August, we scheduled an appointment with the Catholic school principal and kindergarten teacher. I told them that we suspected that Holly might have Asperger's Syndrome, which is like "High Functioning Autism." At that time, I didn't know that some people believe strongly that Asperger's Syndrome is not synonymous with High Functioning Autism.

I asked if the teacher or principal were familiar with Asperger's Syndrome. The kindergarten teacher indicated that, about five years earlier, she had taught a student, who later was identified as having Asperger's Syndrome. They introduced me to a teacher on staff who had a son with Autism. This teacher's son did not attend the school, because he was nonverbal and needed a special program for Autism.

"About how often do you think Holly will require the teacher's individual attention?" The principal asked, at our meeting. "Once per day? Once per hour? More than that?"

"I don't know," I said honestly. "It's a totally new environment. I can't predict how she'll do. She might do just fine, and you might wonder what all this fuss was about, but I can't be sure."

At the same time, we filled out paperwork for the public school in our area. We registered her for the public school kindergarten, in case we ended up deciding that was our best option. We were surprised to find out that, although we had moved fifteen miles from the church, we were not zoned for the public school closest to the church. However, the Catholic schools did not care in which school zone we resided.

We were surprised when Ken's paycheck came and we found that sixty dollars was deducted for "Misc. Deductions." We found out that the office manager had started deducting the Catholic school tuition. "I guess, if they've already started taking the money out for it, maybe we should let her try the Catholic school," I told my mom during one of our phone calls. "I was getting cold feet, but the only real way to know if it will work out, is to try it. I still haven't heard one word from the public school and it will soon be time to get started. The Catholic school kindergarten teacher has about twenty-five years experience, comes highly recommended and seemed nice when we met with her. She wanted to do pre-testing with Holly next week."

After completing the pre-testing, the school still seemed willing to work with us. They said she could have a public school evaluation, while attending there. So, we registered her for kindergarten at the Catholic school. I felt much more comfortable about sending her there, after hearing the teacher say, "She has such a sweet personality."

"Holly is getting nostalgic for her old home and old school," I told Ken one day when he came home from work. "The other day she told me she's moving back to Texas to live with Grandma. When I talk about her new school and new teacher, she asks, 'What about my old school? What about Mrs. Turner?' Today I opened an envelope and she said, 'You did that just like Mrs. Turner.'"

"I know she misses her old school, but she'll adjust," Ken reassured.

The first day of kindergarten arrived. I was concerned to see 27 students in the class, with one teacher and one aid. Holly's non-categorical preschool class fluctuated between eight to ten kids, with a teacher and two aids. "I'm not sure they will be able to handle a kid like Holly, in those circumstances," I told my mom.

I was not encouraged to stay, and I respected the fact that Holly needed to adjust to being at this new school, without mom. At the end of the day, I felt compelled to talk to the teacher about how things went. It was obvious that the school did not want teachers to be "burdened" by daily parent teacher conferences each afternoon. Parents were expected to wait by the main entrance of the school, and let their children come to them. However, I felt my circumstances were unique, and I desperately needed to talk to the teacher.

"Her morning went well, but the afternoon was a little tougher," Mrs. Starr said. "She didn't come in when the recess bell rang. I had to go get her." She seemed surprised; I wasn't. "Is that just her?" She asked. Mrs. Starr seemed worn out and frazzled by the end of the first day. I began to think about our struggle to pay the tuition, combined with the worry that this school was not equipped to meet Holly's needs. I was tempted to bail out, then and there.

"It's only day one," I told myself. "You have to be patient. Besides, we have an evaluation in progress. Let's at least stay long enough to have the evaluation completed."

After her first day in kindergarten, I asked Holly if she had met any friends. She said, "There's lots and lots of them." Then, I remembered that she considered everyone to be her friend. She made no distinctions.

CHAPTER FOURTEEN

We decided against enrolling Shelly in any preschool. She was seven days too young to attend the preschool at the Catholic school. It was probably for the best, since we didn't have the money to send her anyway.

"How would you be able to send her to a regular preschool anyway, since she's not potty trained?" My mom asked.

"I forgot to tell you, she's doing great with that now," I told her. "She says, 'You proud of me?'" All the trauma of failed attempts at training Holly had taken a toll on my confidence. I wasn't sure I was any good at potty training. However, with Shelly, the process was pretty smooth and easy.

As a five year old, Holly went through a phase where her favorite thing was dressing and undressing her toys. I guess she skipped that phase before. I thought we would never get to a point where she was even slightly interested in learning to dress herself, so I decided that dressing her toys was all part of her development. She would bring toys to me that had the clothes sewn on and insist that I cut them off so she could swap them out with another toy's clothes. So, all around our apartment, we had Pooh Bears wearing "ELMO" shirts and kangaroos wearing shirts that said "POOH."

Quite often, she would relentlessly nag me to stop whatever I was doing, and "make a shirt for Pooh," or another toy. Unable to redirect her, or pacify her any other way, I would finally take a little scrap of material and, although I couldn't sew well, I would cut out holes for the arms and neck to slip through. Ken would get home from work and, instead of impressing him by how much unpacking, cleaning or cooking I had gotten done, I only had a few shaggily dressed toys to show for my day's accomplishments. Instead of calling them out-fits, Holly would ask Ken if he liked their new "in-fits."

As a three year old, Shelly became unbelievably verbal. One day I was stressed out and cranky and she looked at me, with a priceless grin, and said, "You so happy! You love me!" She still liked to talk on the phone. When she talked to her Grandma, she would hold the phone away from her mouth and say, "It's your mom."

One day, Holly was shaking her head. Father Ben noticed, and copied her.

"I'm making the room shake," Holly explained.

"Oh?" Father Ben replied. "I didn't know that would make the room shake."

"She tends to have her own perspective on things," I told him. "Last weekend, she wanted to put in an envelope full of small crab apples in the collection at Mass."

"It would have been interesting to see the look you'd get from the ushers," Father commented. She has a uniquely sincere and interesting child-like faith.

In September, Amanda and Dan came to visit us in Michigan. We were riding around Lansing, showing them the sights. Holly kept singing, and making chicken noises. Dan started adding other farm sounds, like "moo" and "oink."

Holly would say, "That's a cow...that's a pig."

Dan tried to fool her by saying, "All right, if you're so smart, what does a kangaroo say?"

Holly thought for a moment and replied, "Well, hello there, Pooh Bear."

One day, when Shelly and I were meeting Holly after school, and waiting for Ken to finish work, so we could all go home, a teacher approached me.

After brief introductions she said, "I notice you're often here after school. We are looking for someone to work in our after school child care program. We are short one person. Would you be interested?" She looked at me, and, as if reading my mind said, "You could bring your kids with you."

Now, I had to think about that. I had become a stay at home mom so that I could be with my kids, but we desperately needed the money. Now, someone was offering me a way to make money, without leaving my kids. Plus, my kids would get to hang out with other kids in the after school care program, without me paying for them to attend. It would be a much better use of our time than just wandering around on the playground, waiting for Ken to finish work.

I discussed, with my new potential employer, my concerns about Holly's special needs, and how they might require my attention while I was supervising other kids. I didn't want to get fired from a job because my daughter was more of a disturbance to the program than I was an asset. "I see her when I'm in the lunch room and lunch recess," she told me. "She does pretty well." She seemed willing to give it a try. I decided this might be what an answer to prayers looks like. I accepted the job and started the next day.

When Holly was going to the Catholic school for kindergarten, occasionally, Ken would be surprised to look up from his desk in his Music Ministry office and see Holly standing there. He would get up and walk her back to class. Usually, the teachers would be in the midst of a frantic search, trying to figure out where she had gone. I believe one time she managed to get to his office and back, before anyone had noticed she was gone. When the thought entered into her mind that she'd like to go see what Daddy was doing, nothing in her mind gave her any cause for hesitation.

Still, I was not fully aware of exactly how separated she was from her peers. One casual conversation with her teacher was very enlightening. "She's so sweet," her teacher began. "One day, Holly was coloring at the table during circle time, and the teaching assistant asked her, 'Wouldn't you like to be with the other kids?' and Holly answered, 'I'm very happy right where I am.' I told my assistant, 'One day you're going to come in here and find me in my happy place.'"

I smiled politely, but I went home and asked Ken, "Why are we struggling to get her to school everyday, if all she is doing is sitting at a table and coloring? I have a table and crayons here at home." It seemed painfully obvious to me that, although she is sweet, and the story was cute, the wrong question had been asked. The staff had presented her with a choice that allowed her to choose what was not in her best interest.

It would have been better if they had said, "It's time for circle time. Do you want to sit in the front or the back?" They could have asked, "Who do you want to sit next to for circle time?" Or, "Do you want to sit on the floor or in a chair?" It was becoming clear to me that, although they had good-intentions, they were ill-equipped and inexperienced in meeting Holly's needs.

Holly's teacher kept in regular contact with me about how she was adjusting. "She seems to be getting along fairly well in the classroom," she told me. "I saw her talking with three girls at her table this morning for awhile, but other than that, she sticks to herself and doesn't socialize."

"Do you think she's following along with the class okay?" I asked.

"She will sometimes come to join our group, and sometimes I see that she's attentive," she replied. "But, I should mention that she will also sometimes leave the room without telling anyone! Mrs. Klein and I will suddenly look at each other and ask, 'Where's Holly?' We've told her she needs to tell someone if she needs to leave, but she hasn't remembered to do that yet."

Holly also struggled with meeting academic expectations, but not due to a lack of capability. "We've had a few coloring assignments," Mrs. Starr said. "The children were to draw a picture of what the sentence is at the bottom. She did draw herself on one of the pages, but didn't really follow the directions. Today, she made pictures of Pooh Bear, which was fine. She asked a boy to help her cut one of them and he cut the legs separate, which she didn't want him to do, and they both got upset!"

Mrs. Starr's father passed away early in the school year. For me, it brought back memories of losing Daddy. Also, death was a subject Holly continued to bring up frequently. It was as if she was trying to get it all figured out. I decided we would go, as a family, to the funeral home to express our condolences to Mrs. Starr. I wasn't going to make a special point of bringing Holly or Shelly to view the body, but it turned out that you couldn't miss it when you first walked in the room. Shelly said, "He's sick."

I told her, "Not anymore. He won't be sick or feel pain anymore. We are happy that he's in heaven, but when you love someone you still miss them when they're gone." We talked about the fact that his body died, but his soul is in heaven.

Holly said, "He didn't take his glasses."

I told her, "He doesn't need his glasses in heaven."

She said, "Let's take his glasses off."

I told her, "No. They want his glasses on, because that's how they remember him." We hugged Mrs. Starr, and she thanked us for coming. She also made a comment about the innocence of children.

At bedtime that night Holly said, "Jesus didn't want those owies. He should have moved his feet away from those pokey things." During bedtime prayers, she fervently prayed, "Dear God, please make Pooh Bear real."

"How's Holly doing lately? Is it working out for her to come with you to your new job?" my mom asked, during our next phone visit.

"After school, she sometimes talks non-stop about a topic of her choice. She particularly likes to go into the parish office where Ken works. Today, she let go of my hand and walked through the Principal's office, the secretary's office and the teacher's lounge to get to the parish office! She likes to go to the office of one of Ken's co-workers because he has an aquarium in there. She interrupts his work and talks his head off about the fish, but when I try to get her to tell me about her school day, she doesn't respond much at all. I feel like I'm in the dark about what goes on with her all day. "

"I'm sure things will smooth out with time," she reassured. "And what about Shelly? How's she doing?"

"Well," I began, "Shelly still cries about not getting to go to Kindergarten. One day this week Holly was whining because I was leaving her and Shelly was crying because I wouldn't leave her. Shelly is very much into the 'I do it myself' phase. On the playground, she almost gives me heart failure. She climbs to the top of the monkey bars.

Sometimes half-way up she lets herself slip through and dangle from her arms. She watches the big kids jump from the tops of the playground equipment, and I can see the gears turning, 'Could I do that too?' That's part of the reason I'm so exhausted today. I try to wear them out and it wears me out instead."

"Well, hang in there!" What more could she say?

The School Psychologist scheduled several interviews with us, as part of Holly's evaluation. He told us that many parents seek the Autism label for their children.

"Why would anyone want their child to be labeled autistic, if they aren't?" I asked.

"Well, in Michigan, they do it for the money."

"What money?" Ken and I asked.

"The government pays families a subsidy to meet the needs of their children with Autism," he explained. "It's meant to enable families to meet the child's needs in the home, rather than having them institutionalized."

"That's the first I ever heard of that," I said. He looked relieved to believe that it was new information to us. Our genuine surprise seemed to encourage him that we had been truthful in our other responses to the interview questions.

The results of the psychologist's evaluation included average intelligence, grade-level academic development, difficulties with social interactions, restricted, repetitive and stereotype patterns of behaviors. "I would view these IQ scores as low estimates of her ability," he told us. "Some days she seemed motivated and very willing to work. Then she performed very well. Other days, she seemed disinterested and didn't do nearly as well. Attention and compliance issues negatively impacted her overall score."

We were told by her evaluators, that during most testing sessions, she would work for 30 minutes. She had a lot of difficulty with visual-motor tasks. She wrote with a "fisted" pencil grasp.

In her responses to questions, Holly sometimes focused on the details and missed the point. When asked what to do if you see a friend crying, she said, "You need to go to your bed if you cry." Non-sensical jargon and delayed echolalic responses were observed by the evaluators, but were infrequent by kindergarten age. Holly's conversational skills were deemed to be parallel, rather than interactive. She had particular difficulty giving meaningful answers to open-ended questions. Her communicative abilities were much better when discussing topics of interest, including her drawings or Winnie the Pooh.

At a meeting with school staff, Mrs. Starr reported that Holly had limited interaction with her classmates. She was slow to engage in classroom activities. She had difficulty with classroom transitions and changing activities.

I had to talk to someone to process all the information I was hearing from the professionals evaluating my daughter. "Amanda," I began when she answered the phone. "Do you remember a long time ago when that nurse first suggested Holly might be 'slightly autistic' and you said that sounded like 'slightly pregnant' and there was no such thing?"

"Yeah," she answered cautiously. "So?"

"Well, do you think that maybe it is possible to be slightly autistic?"

"What do you mean?" she asked.

"They now prefer the term Autism Spectrum Disorders and it is very likely that they may be further divided until many of the conditions that are now called Autism eventually each have their own names."

"Oh?" She prodded.

"One article I read said that they are not sure if it is the same condition in girls as in boys. They are not sure if Asperger's Syndrome and High Functioning Autism are synonyms," I continued.

"So what about Holly?" she asked gently.

"You mean does Holly have one of those things?" I asked.

"Uh-huh."

"The jury is still out. I have learned enough to feel justified in saying that she has some 'autistic tendencies.' I am waiting for an expert to give me a better angle for describing and dealing with her condition. Anyway, I'm trying not to wallow in doom and gloom. She is who she is, and we love her, and we are dealing with her strengths and weaknesses the best we can. Sometimes she brightens our day in the most surprising ways with her witty commentaries."

"Oh yeah?" Amanda encouraged me to continue.

"Yeah, tonight I got home and I called Mama, and I was telling her about the church Barbeque. I told her 'The most aggravating thing for me was that, since it was a party for big kids, they left all the doors open and the teenagers kept running in and out from the church hall to the parking lot and playing in the parking lot. I was afraid they were going to get hit by a car.' Then, Holly, quoted *a Fly Went By,* a Beginners Book by Mike McClintock, saying, 'But that did not stop them. Oh no, not at all!'"

"That's cute," Amanda said.

"My friend was calling me 'remarkable' because I've always managed to keep my sense of humor. But, honestly, with two little stand up comedians like Holly and Shelly running around, who could help having a sense of humor?"

"Why did you call Shelly a comedian?" Amanda asked. "The last time I saw her, she could barely talk."

"She's always grabbing the phone and pretending to talk. It's hilarious to listen to her. And then again, sometimes not so funny. She made me feel guilty one day, when she was jabbering into the phone and then looked at her doll baby and said, 'No, no, baby, I'm too busy.'"

"Now, don't start with the guilt trips. Every mom has to be busy and talk on the phone sometimes," Amanda reassured.

"You know what else is surprising about Shelly?" I asked.

"What?" Amanda asked.

"Well, even through Daddy died before Shelly was born, she's heard Holly talk so much about Papa that she feels like she knows him. She recognizes him on videos and in pictures. She knows that he is in heaven, and that we miss him, but we'll see him some day."

"That's good."

"One day she saw the video with him walking me down the aisle, at our wedding. She said, 'Papa?' I told her yes. She said, 'That's you in heaven?'"

"Oh, that's so sweet." Amanda commented.

CHAPTER FIFTEEN

"You're fat," Holly said bluntly to a classmate, during recess. The girl stood pouting, as she watched Holly walk away. Unlike a child who might say such a thing to provoke a reaction, Holly had no perception of how she had made the other girl feel. She was simply stating, what seemed to her, to be the obvious. She was speaking out loud, the first thought that entered her mind.

Next, Holly walked over, and stood in front of a group of kids. To an observant adult, it seemed obvious that she wanted to play. However, she never told them that she wanted to join in. She seemed clueless about how to jump into the group activity. Then, she began to talk to herself and smile, then laugh and run away.

The Physical Therapist asked to meet with me, after evaluating Holly. "Holly is low-tone and hyper-flexible," she told me.

"What does that mean?" I asked.

"If you look at your arms," she began explaining, "you can see the shape of your muscles. If you look at Holly's arms, everything is soft. Hyper-flexible means her fingers bend too far back, her elbows bend too far. Her knees bend too far. When she tried to do a sit-up, she struggled to get her head off the floor. She needs to have a hand on her thigh to be able to get up from sitting on the floor to a standing position. She has flat feet, which makes it difficult for her to balance, or hop on one foot. She goes upstairs fine without needing a handrail, but to go downstairs, she needs to put both feet on the same step, and use a handrail. She can only keep her feet together to bunny hop for a few repetitions. She can only hop one time on each leg. She can only balance on one leg for 2 or 3 seconds. She is unable to stand with one foot directly in front of the other."

I sat quietly and attentively, trying to take in all the details she was sharing with me. "You were concerned about gross motor skills, right?" she asked. "I'm not shocking you by throwing all this at you, am I?"

"I did have concerns," I responded, still trying to take it all in. "If this means that you are going to be able to help her with all this, then I guess that's good news."

That evening, I tried to explain the physical therapy evaluation results to Ken. "People can say what they want about her behaviors coming from a lack of discipline," I commented, "But I did not parent her into being low-tone and hyper-flexible!" Although I continued to be concerned about Holly's gross motor skills, I took some small comfort in having an objective measure that I had not caused all her problems. I felt some empathy for other parents, dealing with hidden disabilities, with no objective measure to prove that all the problems were not due to parenting.

During the evaluation sessions with the School Social Worker, Holly began making odd noises, before finally indicating that she needed the bathroom. The Social Worker reported that she spent a lot of time in the bathroom, and was singing to herself most of that time.

At the end of the testing session, Holly refused to clean up the toys. "I want to keep playing," she said. The Social Worker succeeded in getting Holly to help clean up, only after making it into a game.

When I was given a copy of the School Social Work Evaluation Report, I read, "Holly's scores on the Child Symptom Inventory met the criterion cutoff scores in the following areas: ADHD, Inattentive type, Motor Tics, Vocal Tics, Autistic Disorder and Asperger's Disorder."

"Unbelievable!" I thought to myself. "Some of those terms I don't even recognize."

"Just remember," the Social Worker explained, "That doesn't mean that she has all of those things. Many of those things share similar characteristics and one disorder rules out the other."

In the conclusion of her report, the School Social Worker wrote, "It is this worker's recommendation that Holly become eligible for special education services, since she has many issues that other children her age do not have to struggle with." I took comfort in the idea that she was trying to obtain help for my child, rather than condemning her behaviors and problems.

The Speech-Language Pathologist administered the Expressive One-Word Picture Vocabulary Test Revised to Holly. The results were a percentile rank of seventy-five and an age-equivalency more than a year above Holly's chronological age. Her vocabulary skills were quite advanced.

The Speech-Language Pathologist noted that Holly tended to obsess about the topic of Ariel, the Little Mermaid. In fact, during one session, the only way she could get Holly to talk was to draw a mermaid and tell Holly, "Ariel lost her voice. She needs you to talk for her." Although Holly was more verbal than her peers, she did not understand turn-taking, change of topic, or questions. She also had difficulty understanding and following oral directions.

The occupational therapist found Holly to be delayed in the areas of fine motor coordination, visual motor skills and visual perceptual skills. She exhibited sensorimotor concerns in the areas of tactile sensation, auditory sensation, olfactory sensation, gustatory sensation, visual sensation, vestibular sensation, muscle tone and coordination. One example of observations of sensory concerns included Holly's sensitivity to sunlight. Holly would put her jacket over her head to block out the sunlight. At recess, she preferred to play in the shade or inside playground tunnels. The occupational therapist also observed Holly licking another child's shirt. She attempted to lick another child's pony tail.

The fact that Holly leaned backward when climbing stairs was deemed to be a sign of vestibular concern. The occupational therapist concluded, "Without proper integration of one's senses, deficits could occur in the following areas: body perception, coordination of both sides of the body, motor planning, activity levels, attention span, emotional stability and perceptual skills."

Holly lost her first tooth in kindergarten. She was trying to open a container and the lid hit her in the mouth, knocking the loose tooth out. She was upset at first, but then she calmed down and was excited about the whole process, including the tooth fairy.

Later that evening, we went back to the church for a social event. We saw a lot of teachers there. Her computer teacher asked her, "Holly, where's your tooth?"

Holly answered, "It's in a bag."

The teacher asked, "What did you do with your tooth?"

"Eat goldfish (crackers)."

"Where did you put the bag?" the teacher asked.

"Under my pillow," she answered.

"Now what's gonna happen?"

"A new tooth is going to come in," Holly told her.

"What else?"

"My other teeth will fall out and new teeth are gonna grow in."

I helped the conversation along a little. "Is that tooth going to stay under your pillow forever?"

"No."

"What's going to happen now?" I asked.

"The tooth fairy's going to come," Holly replied.

"What's the tooth fairy going to leave you?" Her teacher asked.

"A toy Pooh Bear."

"Not that I'm aware of," I silently thought to myself.

At first, Holly's fascination with Winnie the Pooh didn't seem so unusual or obsessive. What kindergartener doesn't like Winnie the Pooh? The first drawings of Winnie the Pooh that she brought home were impressive, based on their artistic merit. It took several days of repeating the pattern, before I commented, "Did you ever notice that every picture she draws is of Winnie the Pooh?"

It was kind of exciting when she first brought home a picture of a mermaid. After all, at least she was no longer fixated on Winnie the Pooh. This time, however, I was quicker to notice the pattern, when all the pictures coming home were mermaids.

One evening, we went to Taco Bell for dinner. As I was staring at the menu, and mentally preparing to give our order, Holly was impatiently tugging at my arm. "What does this say?" She asked, with a strange sense of urgency.

I looked at the container of blue water on the counter, which had caught her attention. "It says 'Make a Wish Foundation.'" I said absent-mindedly.

"I need some money!" She demanded, entranced by the blue-water-Make-A-Wish-Foundation donation container.

Sensing her strong desire, and intrigued by her charitable nature, that she would be so intent to donate to this charity, I began to dig through my pocket until I found a dime. I gave her the dime and watched as she quickly approached the blue water, dropped in her dime and said, "I wish I were a mermaid." She stood completely still, waiting, obviously believing with all her heart, that her wish would be momentarily fulfilled.

I immediately forgot what I needed to order. I was overwhelmed by racing thoughts. First, I was instantly realizing that she was not feeling charitable, and had no idea that she had just donated to a charity. My other thoughts were about child-like faith, which is said to be able to move mountains. I began to wonder what it might look like, if she suddenly turned into a mermaid, right in front of the cash register at Taco Bell. I visualized her dropping to the ground, and flopping her new fins as I screamed, "Get some water!"

One day, we went to the park. Holly started chanting, "Mermaid on the left, bow. Mermaid on the right, sit." She kept repeating it over and over, bowing and sitting, as she said those words. Movie reels began playing through my mind, to see if I could identify where the chant came from. It seemed like *The Little Mermaid* may have said something about "Mermaid off the left bough", but I certainly didn't remember anything about the mermaid on the right.

"Where did you learn that, Holly?" I interrupted her incessant chant. I had to repeat the question a few times, before she responded.

"Uncle Richard," she replied. I asked him later if he ever taught her that chant. He said he didn't think so. He had no memory of ever hearing it before, but he thought it was cute and he was glad Holly remembered him.

The mermaid fixation was strong, but short-lived. In less than six months, unicorns became her topic of obsession. Her love for unicorns seemed to grow stronger, day by day. She once told me that her purpose in life is to make unicorns more popular again. She has repeatedly told me that there will never come a time when she says, "I used to like unicorns."

Uncle Richard and Aunt Carol came to spend our first Thanksgiving in Michigan with us. The girls were so excited by the time they arrived, they could not contain themselves. They kept running around like little pin balls, picking up anything and everything and bringing them over saying, "Look at this." Shelly immediately began showing her cousin, Kevin, (about a year younger than her) all the interesting things to play with.

Holly spent more time discussing with the adults. She walked up to Uncle Richard and Aunt Carol and offered, "Do you want some of my drink?" She passed a soda can toward them and then added, "But never share your germs. Just spit those in the toilet!"

"What's all this Asperger's stuff we've been hearing about Holly?" Richard asked. "We've never noticed anything about her. It can't be that bad. I'm not sure I would agree to let the school slap that label on her."

"Many people would agree with you about avoiding labels," I told him. "But, if you don't know what to call it, how do you know which support group to join? Besides, she may not get the services she needs without a proper diagnosis." I watched him closely, trying to see if I was making any progress with convincing him. "As for why you never noticed it before, we didn't notice it either at first. I'm told that Autism usually gets diagnosed between the ages of 3 and 5 and Asperger's often doesn't get diagnosed until about fourth or fifth grade. Also, Holly does much better relating to adults than peers. One thing that I've noticed is that it doesn't take kids any time at all to figure out that there's something different about her."

"Well, I guess you'll have to see what the experts recommend."

"I'm doing a lot of research and learning a lot," I continued, still trying to convince him.

"Like what?"

"Like these kids have trouble understanding other people's perspectives. Holly has an extremely low frustration tolerance, and then she gets angry or aggressive. Shelly receives the brunt of a lot of Holly's aggression. She might dig her fingernails into Shelly's arm or hit, kick or bite her. One good thing is that Shelly is becoming more verbal, so we can get a better idea of what's going on. We used to hear Shelly cry and, as soon as we walked into the room, Holly would say, 'Nothing happened!!!' Now we hear from Shelly, 'Holly bit my bottom!' Researchers say that, many of the problem behaviors are a result of sensory over-load." We didn't talk much more about it during their visit.

Richard and Carol gave the girls a new Veggie Tale sing-along cassette. It quickly became one of their favorite cassettes to listen to in the car. I played it one night at bed time, but it was pretty up-beat and instead of drifting off to dream land, they got up and started dancing around the room. It was great in the car and, every time Ken turned it down to talk, Holly would say, "Play it loud, please!" Holly and Shelly both excelled at singing along with it.

On Thanksgiving Day, Richard was telling a story about someone at work, who bought a medium sized turkey. Another co-worker had said, "That's not a turkey; this is a turkey!" He mimed the size of the larger bird.

Holly heard the punch line of his story and, without batting an eye, replied, "No, you're the turkey!"

Richard looked at her, astonished. "I walked right into that one!" he exclaimed.

After dinner, we went to a park that had a huge play structure that the kids loved. Shelly loved to climb up every variation of a ladder and slide down all the slides. She made me nervous, but avoided any serious injuries. Once, she lost her footing and just dangled from her arms, until I could get to her, and help her down.

However, parks weren't Holly's favorite things. She didn't like being out in bright sunlight, and she didn't like the slides because the static electricity would shock her. At one point, she found a dad and a little girl, playing with a soccer ball under some shade trees. Then later, when I went looking for her, she was sitting at a picnic table with another family waiting patiently for the food to be served! I told her she needed to come back to her own family. She was not happy with me. The people said, "We were getting worried. She said she didn't know where you were."

"Oh, she knew where we were," I told them. We were at the same table we've been at since we got here. She just thought your food looked better than ours."

"Please don't tell me any horror stories about what could have happened," I told Richard and Carol "because I've already played them all out in my own mind. Sometimes it's just a major challenge to watch them both every minute."

One evening, Richard and Carol treated us to dinner at Chuck E. Cheese. Holly was afraid of the mascot and ran out into the parking lot before we ever made it through the kid-check safety station. I had to carry her back in, against her will. I reassured her that I would be sure Chuck E. stayed far away from her.

"Why are you afraid of Chuck E?" Aunt Carol asked.

"I'm not afraid; it's just too weird." Holly replied.

"What do you mean by that?" Uncle Richard asked.

"That's not really a mouse," Holly explained. "I like for humans to look like humans. It's really just a stranger in there." I decided the mascot costume must make her wonder what the person was trying to hide. I compared it to the scene in movies, when someone walks into a convenience store, wearing a ski mask.

Shelly and the others had a lot of fun going crazy in there. The worker misunderstood and thought we were celebrating Shelly's birthday, so he gave her a little paper crown and a balloon. For days, Shelly kept saying, "Chuck E. gave these to me. Chuck E. loves me."

One morning at breakfast, Aunt Carol gave Holly a doughnut hole. Uncle Richard kept saying, "Don't eat that. It's yucky! You better let me eat it."

I kept eating one, and he was eating another one, and I kept telling her, "It's good. Uncle Richard's just teasing you." She kept looking back and forth from him to me, trying to make sense of it all. After they went home, I offered her another one and she took it hesitantly saying, "Uncle Richard says it's yucky."

CHAPTER SIXTEEN

Holly was doing what most moms recognize as the "potty dance." I asked her, "Do you need to go potty?"

She said, "No, I'm just jumping with glee."

Holly and Shelly immensely enjoyed having family visiting. When Uncle Richard and Aunt Carol were packing up to leave on Sunday, Holly said, "I thought you were going to live with us."

"Oh, no, honey. We have to go back to our own home. We have jobs to go back to."

Then Holly said, "Someday you'll move to Michigan." She always seemed to be strategizing about how to get her long-distance extended family to live in one place.

Holly's sleep issues had not resolved themselves by kindergarten age. She simply seemed more capable of defeating any tactic we tried. She was harder to restrain, and was frequently content to be left alone. One night, I decided, "That's it. I'm going to put her in her room, and leave her there until she falls asleep, no matter how long she screams and cries!"

I put her in her room, read her a story, sang a song, kissed her goodnight and turned off the light. Almost immediately, I heard her get out of bed. Then, from under the door, I saw the light come on. I told her firmly that she was to stay in her room. I held the door shut, until she lost interest in the door, and became interested in some toys and books. She happily entertained herself for four hours before finally giving in to sleep.

By that time, I knew of other families who used medication to help their children get to sleep. I was beginning to think it was the only way. I discussed it with Holly's pediatrician. He stated that he was not comfortable medicating a 5 year old for sleep and that if that's what she needed, he would refer to a psychiatrist.

I asked if he had any suggestions about what we should do. He told me that children with autism would prefer to operate on a thirty hour day. His suggestion was, "Try to get her to sleep fifteen minutes earlier. Then, after she adjusts to that, get her to sleep fifteen minutes earlier than that. Keep continuing until you train her to go to sleep at the normal time." The advice pacified me long enough to get me out of his office, but it was ineffective in implementation. I could never figure out how to get her to sleep fifteen minutes earlier so the process stopped at step one.

I learned that there are things within my control, and there are things that are out of my control. Sometimes there are things that we are unsure about whether or not we control. I learned that I could force Holly into her room, or into her bed, but I couldn't force her to sleep. During potty training, I learned that I could force her to "sit," but I couldn't force her to "go." When Amanda told me that the psychologist she worked with had explained that parents can't control their child's bodily functions, that rang true with me.

We noticed that, although Holly slept soundly once sleep was initiated, it did not seem to be typical sleep. Anyone sleeping near her was likely to be on the receiving end of multiple kicks and arm flailing. We soon gave up on the twin bed for her, because she needed a full size bed to give her more room to thrash around and turn upside down. And of course, in the morning she seemed to be comatose. We commented that we would need a crane to lift her out of bed.

On the rare nights that Holly did wake up during the night, it was as if she had reverted to infancy. She seemed to have lost all ability to communicate. She would cry, scream and kick, but not let us know, verbally or through gestures, what the problem was. Eventually, we learned that the problem was frequently that she needed to use the bathroom. Instead of just getting up and going to the bathroom, she would scream and cry until we would carry or pull her to the bathroom, undress her and sit her on the toilet. Then she would relieve herself, and stumble back to bed and to sleep.

Again, we worried about what types of abuse the neighbors might have imagined that we were inflicting on her. Sometimes we would maneuver her all the way to the bathroom, only to learn that our hypothesis was wrong. She had not awakened because she needed to use the bathroom. Perhaps it was a nightmare that woke her, or she was too hot, or sick. Then, on top of whatever problem had awakened her, she would also be furious about being hauled to the bathroom, and placed on the toilet for no good reason.

I attended a parent group, at which another family told me that they had used melatonin to help their sons on the spectrum get to sleep at night. I called the pediatrician's office and they would neither condone nor condemn it. They said that, since it is not a drug, there is no empirical evidence to prove or disprove its effectiveness, or even safety.

I called the pharmacy and was told that they could not recommend it for anyone under age 18 and it "probably wouldn't help anyway." Out of desperation, we tried a low dose. Instead of a four hour battle to get her to sleep, she made a smooth transition to sleep two hours after taking the melatonin. I don't think I slept at all for the first few nights because I didn't know what the effects might be, and I wanted to be sure I was awake to rush her to the emergency room at the first sign of trouble. When Holly was taking melatonin, it was the first time in her life that I ever saw her fall asleep watching a movie.

Eventually, with enough persistence on my part, I convinced the pediatrician to order a sleep study for Holly. The sleep study involved Holly and me spending the night in a hospital room. She had numerous sensors attached to various body parts from head to toe. She questioned the technician before each sensor was placed. The technician was exceedingly patient, as she answered each question and assured Holly that none of those things were going to hurt. The equipment monitored Holly's heart rate, brain rhythm and breathing all night long. They also video-taped her while she was sleeping.

We arrived at the hospital at eight PM. There was a VCR in the room, but I knew that Holly was not likely to fall asleep watching a movie. Instead, I brought a stack of books to read. I read and read to her, until my eyes were barely open and I feared losing my voice. At last, she fell asleep. I looked at my watch. It was midnight.

At our follow-up appointment with the pediatrician, he told us that the sleep study showed no signs of sleep apnea. "It says here that you could have a referral to a sleep medical specialist, if you want," the doctor reported.

"Then, I guess we want that," I replied. "I need to find something to help her to get a better night's sleep."

The sleep medicine specialist diagnosed Holly with Delayed Sleep Phase Syndrome. Once again, my daughter had a syndrome that I had never heard of. The doctor asked, "Does this sound like what's going on? She can't get to sleep at a normal time, but, once she falls asleep much later, she sleeps soundly, but she can't wake up when she's supposed to because she hasn't gotten enough sleep. If she is allowed to sleep as long as she wants, she'll sleep quite late, but then she'll feel fine when she wakes up. So the cycle of staying up late and having trouble waking up in the morning keeps continuing. Is that right?"

"Yeah," I agreed. "You just described our life."

"This condition is genetic," the doctor continued. "It's not about your parenting or her choosing not to go to bed. Her inner clock is programmed to fall asleep at a much later time. In caveman times, she would have been the one designated to stay up to make sure the campfire didn't go out. The problem is, her sleep pattern is not very conducive to the type of schedule she's expected to keep in our society today."

It didn't sound like there was likely to be a simple solution, but I was relieved to sense that the doctor grasped what we were dealing with and didn't seem to be blaming us. The doctor said that it was quite likely that Holly truly wished she could fall asleep when everyone wanted her to. She was probably as frustrated as we were and was wondering what was wrong with her.

"By this time," the doctor continued explaining, "it is no longer only physical; it has also become psychological. The bedroom, which should be a calm and relaxing place, has, for Holly, become a torture chamber of nightly conflict." I hadn't thought of our struggles to get Holly to sleep as being torment for her as well.

"There are three options for dealing with Delayed Sleep Phase Syndrome," the doctor surmised. "The first option is to struggle. That's what you're doing now. That's where she stays up late and everyone is miserable, then she doesn't want to get up on time and everyone's miserable, then she's tired and crabby during the day and everyone stays miserable until time to start the cycle over again the next bedtime." I wondered if he had cameras hidden in our walls. It was uncanny how accurately he was describing our situation.

"Option two is to try to change the world. That's where you work with the school to let her start her day later and you continue letting her fall asleep later and get up later. It may be very expensive for the school because they may have to order internet courses or something to provide for educational opportunities later in the day. I have several patients whose school day starts at noon and I have one patient whose school day starts at three PM."

In the public school system, general education kindergarten was a half day program. Therefore, I felt like anything she got in the morning was extra. "The third option is to use a combination of medication and behavior modification to try to adjust Holly's sleep cycle. It isn't easy and it's not going to change her natural inclination to fall asleep later, but it may help her get through her school years. As an adult, she may very well choose to work the night shift.."

The doctor prescribed medication, which was melatonin-based, and was meant to make transitioning to sleep easier. "No medicine is going to work like magic. I'll refer you to a book to read about things you can do at home, things like turning all the lights down low in the evening and exposing her to bright light in the morning. I'll write a letter to her school telling them not to penalize her for being tardy and to consider a later start time for her school day. They can put that in her IEP. If we can't make some improvements, I can refer you to a sleep psychologist." I didn't even know there was such as thing as a sleep psychologist.

A few days later, after giving Holly her bedtime medicine, I was trying in vain to get Holly to lie down and attempt to fall asleep. She said, "It's no use. No medicine is going to work. The doctor said so."

Holly's experience in a general education kindergarten with limited support continued to be rocky at best. Her teachers tried, and truly seemed to have her best interest at heart. However, just like us, they were fumbling along, without exactly knowing what they were doing.

"She's so funny," the school secretary told me one day. "I saw her walking down the hall in line, with her class. I looked down at her feet, and she only had one shoe on. I asked her, 'Holly where's your other shoe?' It had fallen off way back there and she just kept walking."

One day Holly came home wearing a different shirt than she had worn to school. I always sent a spare set of clothes in her book bag, just in case. "Holly, what happened to the shirt you were wearing this morning?" I asked.

"It got wet," she answered nonchalantly.

"So who helped you change your shirt?" I knew she didn't change clothes independently.

"The teacher."

"Did she take you in the bathroom to change your shirt?"

"No, the hallway," she replied casually. I could picture the whole scene in my mind. Holly's shirt got wet, probably from the water fountain. Holly did not like having wet clothing on, so she immediately pulled it off. In a panic, the teacher probably hurried to get another shirt on her, as quickly as possible. For Holly, it was no big deal.

Another day, a teacher saw me after school and said "I thought you should hear this from me before you hear it from the other kids." I braced myself for the news that would be forthcoming. "Holly was naked in the hallway today."

"What?!?" I exclaimed.

"She didn't make it to the bathroom in time. She left her wet clothes in the bathroom and walked out in the hallway to her book bag to get her change of clothes. My second grade class was out in the hallway, lining up for the water fountain. One of my students said, 'There's a naked girl in the hallway!' I hurried over to Holly and helped her back in the bathroom and helped her get changed. I told her she needs to change her clothes in the bathroom."

"Oh my, thank you for your help," I stammered.

"That's all part of being a teacher," she replied graciously.

I related the incident to my co-worker with the after school care program. I was quite embarrassed, but I needed to tell someone, just to process the event in my own mind. She said, "Some people are very comfortable with their bodies and walk around naked all the time at home. If that's how they feel, I say 'more power to 'em.'" I wondered if she thought that I walk around naked at home and that Holly was copying that example.

"Who built the ark?" Holly began singing one evening. "No one. No one," she continued. Oh boy. I thought she had really learned something from that song, but that certainly wasn't the intended message.

"Listen to Mommy sing it," I coached. "Who built the ark? Noah! Noah," I sang. "His name was Noah. Noah built the ark!"

With encouragement from Holly's evaluation team, we began exploring available options for educational programming. Should we leave her in this kindergarten class? Certainly, people were kind to her here. I loved when she came home singing new songs about Jesus that she had learned. However, she could not have paraprofessional support within this classroom. The Catholic school couldn't afford to hire a one on one paraprofessional, and the public school could not send one into a parochial classroom.

Eventually, we felt like the decision was made for us. Holly got frustrated when a girl in class called her a "baby," so Holly bit the girl. The next day I received a call from the school principal. "I just wanted to check with you to see how you handled this from home."

I was a little taken aback by the inquisition. What was she hoping to hear from me? Did she want me to say that I spanked her? I've tried spanking Holly for behavior infractions, and it has never improved her behavior. Did she want me to say that we grounded her? Holly barely understands the link between cause and effect, behavior and consequence. She would not understand the concept of grounding. Besides, she is so stuck in the here and now, it would be difficult for her to understand why she was being punished for something she did hours ago.

"Well," I began uncomfortably, "we talked to her, and we told her that biting is unacceptable. We told her that animals bite when they get upset, but that people don't bite. We told her she has to use her words to express her frustration and that she can't bite anyone."

"We don't even know if that talk is going to work," the principal replied. "We have no way of knowing whether or not she will do this again." My heart was sinking as I continued to ask myself what response she could possibly want from me. "I know you were checking into the public school in your area. I was wondering how that was going." There was a pause and then she added, "If I was in your shoes, and she was my child, I would want her in a program where they could meet her needs as soon as possible." Her words landed on me like an avalanche. I felt as though Holly had just been expelled.

I don't even know what words I said to end the painful telephone call, because it was as if I was having an out of body experience. I immediately called the public school and asked to speak with that principal. By the time she answered the phone, I was crying and couldn't speak.

"I'm sorry," I wept, "I'm just a little emotional."

"Oh, I'm sorry," the bewildered principal replied, clueless about who I was and why I was calling.

"We live in your school district and my daughter, who has Autism, is going to kindergarten at a Catholic school. She bit someone in her class and now they don't want her there anymore. My husband and I would like to come visit your school and see about moving her there."

CHAPTER SEVENTEEN

The public school principal graciously arranged a time for us to come and tour the school and meet one of the special education teachers, Mrs. Wright. Before that visit, I told Ken, "Our job today is to go and fall in love with this school, and fall in love with these teachers." I felt like this school was our last hope. If it didn't seem like the right place for Holly, I didn't know what I would do. Fortunately, we were so warmly welcomed and reassured that they could help us with Holly, that our job was very easy.

The new school said that their schedule was currently being disrupted by half-days for parent-teacher conferences. They suggested that Holly transition there the next week.

"I feel like the other school doesn't want her anymore," I answered honestly. "And I don't want her to spend one minute where she is not wanted. If you don't want her to start here until next week, I'll gladly keep her home, but I don't want to send her back to that school."

"No, no," Mrs. Wright quickly revised her position, "We can make arrangements for her to start here right away. We don't want her to stay home for a week."

I went back to the Catholic school to let them know that Holly would not be completing the year there. As I neared the principal's office, I overheard the guidance counselor reassuring the principal, "If we let her stay here, we would not be doing what is best for the child. We are ill-equipped to meet her needs." It annoyed me that this conversation was occurring without my input, and that they were so confident that they understood what was best for my child, better than me.

I told the principal that we would be moving Holly to the other school. Her response surprised me. I thought I would see relief on her face. Instead, I saw concern. "What I don't want to happen," she began "is for you and Ken to decide to move her over a weekend and then the other kids don't get a chance to tell her goodbye."

I called the public school back and told them that we agreed to let Holly finish the week at the Catholic school. Everyone in her class made her a card wishing her well in her new class.

"I refuse to let Holly believe that she was kicked out of that school!" I told Ken.

"So what are you going to tell her?" He asked.

"I'm going to tell her, 'You've already learned everything that you were supposed to learn at that school, so we're taking you to a new school, with a special program, that will be able to teach you new things.'" That's what I told her and it allowed her to start at the new school with a positive attitude.

"Hi, I'm Heather," a friendly lady said, on Holly's last day at the parochial school. "You're Holly's mom, aren't you?"

"Yes," I replied.

"My daughter is in the same class with Holly," she said.

"Oh. Well, actually, this is Holly's last day in that class," I explained.

"Oh, really? Why?" she asked.

"Well," I searched for an explanation. "We found out she has an Autism Spectrum Disorder known as Asperger's Syndrome, and we're moving her to a public school where she can get more services."

"Really?" Heather replied, surprised. "I'm a speech-therapist in the public schools. I work with kids with Asperger's. I have a strong interest in that."

"Really?" Now I was surprised. "I'm a speech therapist too. I just haven't been working for the past few years because I've been staying home with my kids."

"You're a speech therapist?" Heather exclaimed. "We're looking to hire a part-time speech therapist. Would you be interested?"

"I don't know," I hesitated. How had a casual conversation with a fellow parent suddenly turned into a job offer?

Heather encouraged me to apply for the two and a half day a week position. I would be working the same number of hours that I was working at the after school care program, but I would be making more money. I wouldn't be able to take my kids with me, but Holly would be in school and Shelly would be ecstatic to go to day care. Besides, I wouldn't be able to continue my work at the after school care program now that Holly would no longer be going to that school. I typed up a resume and completed the interview process. Before I knew it, I was a school-based speech-language pathologist again.

At the Catholic school, kindergarten had been a full day. At the public school, kindergarteners typically went for half a day. The public school told us that, due to Holly's needs, they could program a full day for her.

Within the first week, I received a phone call from Mrs. Wright, the new Special Ed. teacher. "Mrs. Kennedy, we have been noticing that Holly does quite well with all the academic tasks. She doesn't need any remediation with academics. When kindergarten students come to school for a full day, we usually spend half a day working on remediation skills. Since she doesn't seem to need that, we were wondering if maybe you'd like to spend a little more time with her at home. How would that work with your schedule?"

I was getting used to the story changing every time Holly spent a few days in a classroom. It seemed teacher's first impressions of her were quick to change. People even referred to it as the honeymoon phase. "I'm not concerned about my work schedule," I began, "And I would love to spend more time with Holly, but I'm a little concerned about the idea of her only going half days. Holly has been going to school for full days since she was three years old. I think it might be a little strange for her to switch to half days now. Plus, I think we might have difficulty switching back to full days next year."

"Well, that's true. We weren't looking at it like that."

"I'm also wondering," I continued, "If she's getting pulled out for physical therapy, occupational therapy, speech therapy and to work with the social worker, how much time would she actually be in that kindergarten room, if she were only going to school half a day?"

"Well, that's true too. I could definitely have all of her related services pull her out of our room in the morning. Then she could stay all afternoon in the kindergarten room."

"I'm also thinking that part of the reason she's doing so well at your school might be that she gets to slowly transition into her day by starting in a small group setting before going into the regular kindergarten class," I concluded. We agreed that she would continue to go for full days. A few days later they told me that they had added Holly to a first grade math group in the resource room, because she was demonstrating competency with the first grade skills.

Since most kindergarten students were not at school during lunch, due to the half day schedule, they also had Holly go to a first grade classroom to eat her lunch. One day, I went to the school to volunteer. The kindergarten teacher, Mrs. Davis, gave me a job to do in the teacher workroom, which was also the room where several teachers were eating their lunch. I heard one teacher, whom I did not know, say to another teacher, "Well, I lost Holly today."

I immediately turned around from the project I was working on. "Would that be my Holly?" The teacher stared at me like a deer in headlights. "Holly Kennedy?" I asked.

She nodded. It turned out that she was the first grade teacher for the class where Holly ate her lunch. During the lunch hour, Holly decided to leave, so she left.

At home, we learned the scary way that we continued to need to have "child-proof doorknobs" on almost every door of our home. One day, prior to the installation of the child-proof doorknobs in the new apartment, Holly opened the door and let two year old Shelly out of the apartment. Then, she left also, and walked in an opposite direction! I wished at least one of my children would have "known better." Another day, she opened the apartment door and let Shelly out (Shelly was unable to open doors by herself). Holly then closed the door, and sat back down and continued watching TV.

We enjoyed several months of no escapes with the plastic door knob covers, but I became nervous when I found the door to the computer room open, when I was sure I had latched it. I realized that, if she had learned to open that door, then there was nothing to stop her from leaving home. I began the process of asking the apartment complex if we could install the type of bolt locks that require a key to open from each side.

The school was able to implement many strategies to help Holly learn social norms and expectations. One of the first strategies was to post a stop sign on classroom doors to remind Holly not to leave without permission. They also printed one for us to hang on our apartment door at home. I knew that Holly understood what the sign meant, when I saw her remove the stop sign before sneaking out through the apartment door. When we talked about the purpose of the stop sign, Holly replied, "I just don't always follow that rule."

The school also sent home social stories which promoted positive social and behavior skills. We faithfully read all of her social stories each night before bed. One story, which was about getting along with your sister in the car, had Shelly's name in it. After we had been reading the stories for about a month, Shelly noticed her name in that story.

"That's me," Shelly exclaimed!

"No, it's not!" Holly corrected.

Confused, I responded, "Yes, it is."

Surprised, Holly asked, "You mean these stories are about me?" I wanted to hit my head against a brick wall. I couldn't believe we had been reading these stories every night for a month and she didn't even know they were about her. I felt like we might as well have been reading nursery rhymes.

When Holly would talk to me about recess, I noticed that she always talked about the kids who pushed her on the swing, but never mentioned taking a turn to push. "Do you ever push your friends on the swing?" I asked one day.

"No," she answered emphatically.

"Well, you should offer to push them sometimes. Kids don't like to always be the one pushing you. They'd like you to offer to push them once in awhile."

"But it's not nice to push people," she responded. I wondered how she would ever make sense of our world.

The music teacher announced that they would be forming a volunteer choir that would meet during one recess per day. They would be able to perform at the zoo during the Christmas season. The students were asked to raise their hands if they were interested.

I read the paper about the volunteer choir when it came home in Holly's book bag. "Did you volunteer for the choir?" I asked.

"No," Holly replied.

"Really?" I asked, surprised. "But you love to sing!"

"But my voice might get tired from singing and my feet get tired from walking around the zoo."

"Honey, I don't think your voice would get tired and I don't think you need to worry about your feet getting tired at the zoo. I think you would enjoy being in the choir."

On Friday, which was a couple of days later, Holly regretted that she had not volunteered for the choir. "I meant to say yes, but I made a mistake and said no." She asked me how to spell various words so that she could write a note to the music teacher about her mistake. She was frustrated when she realized she would not be able to give the note to the music teacher until Monday. Eventually, the music teacher called me and said that Holly had not missed the deadline to join the choir. She was happy to accept Holly into the choir.

One night, Holly was happily eating the dinner that Ken had prepared. It was a Cajun recipe that Uncle Dan had shared with us. Holly asked, "Is this gumbo?"

"No," I answered, "It's called dirty rice."

"Yuck!" She exclaimed. Appalled, she immediately put her fork down like she wasn't going to eat any more.

"It's not actually dirty," I explained. "That's just a nick-name."

"I don't like yucky rice."

"It's not yucky rice. And it's not dirty. They just call it that because it's brown."

"Can I call it butterfly rice?" she asked. "That's a funny nick-name." I told her that would be fine. Just then, Shelly indicated that she wanted down from her high chair. As I lifted her to the floor, it was obvious she was wearing most of her dinner.

"Take my off," Shelly requested, raising her hands above her head.

"You're so cute!" I said, as I pulled the shirt over her head, and went to get a clean one.

"I so tute?" she repeated with her developmentally acceptable "t" for "k" substitution.

"Now that's cute!" I silently thought. "It's no wonder that Holly gets jealous, thinking that no one thinks her mistakes are as adorable as Shelly's."

Although Holly was only in kindergarten, she had so many adults working with her, it was difficult to keep track. It was also difficult to know how to talk to Holly about all her service providers. It seemed strange to ask, "Did you see your social worker today?" Fortunately, Holly figured out the solution to that problem for herself. She recognized that she had math teachers, spelling teachers, music teachers, etc.. She began to call her social worker "fun teacher" because she was the one who was teaching her how to play!

In the special education resource room, Holly worked with a male paraprofessional in a math group. An adjustment was made to the paraprofessionals' schedules. Someone else took over the math group and Mr. Robinson began supervising, in her classroom, during the lunch hour. Holly came home and said, "Mr. Robinson used to be the math teacher, but now he's the lunch teacher." It sounded like a major demotion.

Holly brought home a math worksheet. I told her we needed to do her homework. She seemed to become defiant saying, "That's not homework; that's free draw."

I told her that we needed to do it, but she flatly refused. Eventually, I gave up and sent a note to the teacher explaining why it was not complete. The teacher wrote a note back saying that it was a recycled math sheet provided for coloring at recess time. Holly was right; it wasn't homework. I was exasperated wondering how I would help Holly conform to expectations when I didn't understand them myself.

We always had behavior issues with Holly while riding in the car. It didn't seem to make much difference if we were going on a long trip, or just around the corner. Although Shelly started out in life as a timid, complacent little one, she was not about to grow up as Holly's punching bag. So, before long, we found ourselves driving down the road with a kick boxing match going on in the back seat. They would also kick the car doors or the seats in front of them. They would use loud and/or annoying noises, progressing to verbal arguments that often led to pinching, scratching hitting or throwing toys.

Shelly could not keep up with Holly in a verbal argument. So, she was frequently the first one to go to blows. I have blocked out the exact number of times that I was horrified to turn around and see that Holly had unbuckled Shelly's car seat at the base where it was attached to the car. I think the behaviors were worse in the car because mom and/or dad were busy driving, and it was not as feasible to use techniques like time-out to control the behavior.

We would try pulling over and leaving one of the girls in the car seat for time-out, while we stood in the parking lot, but it didn't seem to be effective. We also tried proactive approaches, such as singing "quiet voices in the car...." which seemed to help some, but it required us to focus our sole attention on the behavior strategy, and often the relief was short-lived. We wondered if having a conversation, as we drove down the road, was just too much to hope for.

After discussing it at our parent support group meeting, we got more suggestions from other parents who had "been there." Some of the ideas that helped were listening to stories on audio cassette, with or without headphones, having pictures in the car of where we were going, singing or listening to favorite songs and having special toys that were only used for car trips. Of course, when the thrill of those toys wore off, we had to rotate with new ones. It also helped if Holly and Shelly had a snack or drink in the car. Eventually, we invested in a portable DVD player for longer trips. Although it wouldn't have been my first choice, it came to a point that we decided it was important for our sanity, blood pressure and overall driving safety.

Once we started using Velcro to attach pictures of where we were going to the visor of the car, Holly quickly learned the system well enough to manipulate it. If we posted the schedule, "post office, grocery store, McDonalds," then, while we had our backs turned, Holly would climb out of her car-seat and re-arrange the pictures, so that McDonalds was first on the list.

As the winter weather approached, I got a note from Mr. Robinson saying that Holly needed some gloves as her hands were getting quite cold at recess. I was surprised and frustrated to read the note since Holly's coat pockets had contained gloves for several weeks and there was a hat in her book bag. I could not believe that she was freezing every day at recess because she did not know to check her pockets, nor did the adults working with her.

We received a notice from the school that Holly had failed a vision screening. The note said that Holly had reported that she has glasses, but doesn't wear them. I contacted the school to clarify that the only glasses she had were non-prescription sun-glasses and that she had passed her last vision exam at the eye doctor's office. I asked whether she had understood the vision screening task. We took her back to the ophthalmologist and found that her vision was almost exactly the same as it had been two years earlier and she did not require glasses.

CHAPTER EIGHTEEN

"Has anyone else ever been told, or experienced the phenomenon, that your child's behavior is better when you're not around?" I asked at a parent support group meeting. "My daughter's preschool teacher last year told us that Holly's behavior at school was better when we were not there. She attributed it to 'inconsistencies' in our parenting style and said that we give Holly 'too many chances' before consequences. It made me feel like a bad mom."

"Jake's behavior is definitely better at school than at home, or with others rather than with me," one mom volunteered. "I think the reason for this is that he feels more comfortable with me, and knows that I'll love him, no matter what he does. At school, he has to hold it together, because he doesn't know how they'll react if he looses control."

"Our son has always felt safer to let it all out around us," another mom agreed. "When we go to functions, he is one of the better behaved kids around, but when he's at home, he needs the time to let loose and release his anxiety."

"Our kids work so hard at keeping it together at school that they need to release when they come home," another mom passionately chimed in. "Mom is the one person they trust to always love them, no matter what. They trust us to be there for them, even when they are totally out of control. If she's letting go with you, she feels safe with you. As big a pain as it is when our kids are like that, it shows you have a wonderful connection with her."

"What right does that teacher have to accuse you of being inconsistent anyway?" another parent objected. "She should realize that you are constantly trying to adapt to the needs of your child. Gees, I wish people would think, before they open up their mouths, and say something like that!"

"You should go and see a geneticist," a nurse told me, after listening to some of the issues we were dealing with. I was hurt and offended.

My feeling was, "We are interested in helping the child that we have. We are not interested in being told, 'Don't reproduce again.'" I am glad we didn't know about the problems Holly would have, before she was born. I definitely do not regret having her. Her life has a purpose, and I believe the world is better for her presence in it. I know my life is richer for having her in our family.

We already had our second child, before we had detected Holly's disability, so we didn't have this consideration then. Still, Ken and I had always planned to have more than just two children. Now we faced the question of, "Do we limit our family size, for fear of having another child with high needs?"

The concern was legitimate. Holly could certainly be "high-maintenance" on a frequent basis. Being a good mom required a lot of consistent energy and effort. I was often left feeling exhausted. I sometimes wondered, "How could I handle another child who needed me this much?"

Still, my heart, and my faith, reassured me that God wouldn't send more than I could handle. I believe that when God sends a child, He also sends the grace necessary to meet that child's needs. Although, He stretches us past what we believe is our limit.

One Saturday, Ken was on his way to accompany and sing at a wedding, when the car sputtered to the side of the road. Apparently, the drive from Texas to Michigan had taken its toll on the hunk-of-junk, and there was no repairing her. Ken had to temporarily abandon the car, on the side of the road, and call for a taxi to rush him to the church. By the time he arrived, the bride was in a panic over the fact that her music minister had not shown up.

After his Saturday work obligations, he had the car towed to a dealership. After several days of frustrating negotiations, we closed a deal on a used car, with our nonfunctional car as a trade-in. The interest rate was atrocious, but desperate times called for desperate measures.

"No! No!" Holly wailed. "But what about our old car? I miss our old car." I was so fed up with the old car, that it was difficult to have empathy for her reaction. Still, I recognized that she was having difficulty with yet another transition, and coping with change. I recognized her need to grieve.

"I'm sorry you're sad," I told her. "I know you miss the old car. I'm sure we will all miss some things about the old car, but there are good things about the new car too." Under my breath, I muttered, "For instance, it drives!"

I began noticing that, every time I talked to my mom on the phone, she sounded lonely and depressed. I felt bad for moving away from her, and taking her precious grandbabies. Finally, I said, "I wish I could offer you more, but all I can offer is a bedroom, if you want to come and live with us."

I was surprised when she responded, "You don't have an extra bedroom."

"Well, we could make room for you," I began. "If Holly and Shelly shared a room, then you could have the third bedroom."

"That's the best prospect I've heard yet!" She said excitedly.

"Ken," I said, when we had finished our phone call. "I just invited my mom to move in with us." We were both surprised that she was truly considering it. It would have been presumptuous for us to think we could just pick up and move and she would follow us, wherever we went. Yet, she seemed to be missing us so much, that it was just the invitation she was looking for.

She put her house on the market, put some things in storage, and made arrangements to make Michigan her new home. Richard and Carol and Amanda and Dan all played a part in helping her get organized for the move.

Holly managed to charm her way into the hearts of many staff members of the new school. When Mr. Robinson was assigned to walking her through the lunch line, he told me that she always told him what she had decided to eat, as they walked down the hall.

"I think I'll have chicken nuggets," she'd say.

"Yes, Your Highness," he'd reply. I thought it was cute that he called her "Your Highness." I think it may have had something to do with the way she used verbal communication beyond her years. If I had detected any scorn in the way he said it, I would have been insulted, but he seemed to truly be admiring Holly.

One day, she told him, "Why do you call me 'Your Highness?' I prefer to be called just Holly." So, that was the end of her royal reign.

Mr. Robinson was even gracious enough to forgive her, when she took the popcorn that he had prepared for his lunch. She saw the bag of popped popcorn on the kitchen counter near the resource room, so she proceeded to fill herself a bowl. The teachers explained to her that she wasn't allowed to do that. When they told Mr. Robinson about it, he just asked, "Why did I leave it there in the first place?"

One evening, I was trying to do some work for my job, and the girls kept interrupting. The more Ken tried to redirect them, the more irritated they were getting with him for "running interference," and keeping them from me. Frustrated, he told Holly, "I'm just trying to keep you out of Mommy's hair."

Holly loudly protested, "I'm not doing anything to Mommy's hair!"

In contrast, on another evening, I was working at the computer, when I heard Holly casually enter the room. I saw her through my peripheral vision, but I didn't turn to scrutinize her. I kept my focus on my word processor document, until I felt a slight tug at my hair and heard a distinct snip. I turned around, shocked to see she had just cut a lock of my hair.

Holly cried when two fish from her aquarium died. We finally got her to calm down and go to sleep. The next morning, Holly told me that she had dreamed it was Mrs. Wright's birthday. "We were having a party at school. We were doing art with fabric and strings. There was a pool filled with water at recess."

When she got home that afternoon, Mrs. Wright had written a note about her day. The note indicated that Holly had been defiant all morning and then quiet and sullen all afternoon. She had been in time-away three times during the day, for refusing to follow directions. Mrs. Wright wrote, "Yikes! She didn't want to do anything we asked. She wouldn't say the pledge, do her work, or stay in her seat." I wondered if her dream made her think that it was supposed to be a party day, and not a work day.

She came home wanting to go to the pet store and buy some new fish. I told her, "It's not a good day to go to the pet store to buy new fish, when you chose time-away three times at school."

Not making any connection in her mind between what happened at school and what was happening now, Holly cried, complaining, "It is a good day!"

"Maybe tomorrow will be a better day," I offered.

"Tomorrow will not be a better day," she insisted. "Tomorrow will be a worser day!"

Shelly announced one day, "Mice go poop."

Holly said, "No, mice go 'squeak, squeak, squeak.'"

I quickly left the room so that the girls would not see my stifled laugh. A few minutes later, I heard Shelly crying. I returned to see Holly physically blocking Shelly from walking to me. Holly kept screaming, "I'm sorry! I'm sorry! I'm sorry!" I moved Holly out of the way so that I could pick Shelly up, but Shelly was unable to explain what had happened. I knew that some day Shelly would have the verbal skills to explain their frequent conflicts, but for the time being all I could do was play the role of prosecuting attorney with Holly in the role of hostile witness.

At a demonstration for some professional quality cookware, I saw someone cook a pineapple upside down cake in a nonstick skillet on a stove-top burner, and then just flip it out of the pan. Grandma bought the new skillet for us. So, we decided to try the stove-top upside down cake, but we didn't have a recipe to follow to know how long to cook, or how high the burner should be set.

Shelly, didn't like chocolate, so she was excited to help me make lemon cake batter. We started cooking it on medium heat on the burner, but didn't know how to tell when it was done. By the time we took it off the burner we had a charbroiled cake that came cleanly out of the nonstick fry pan. Shelly took one look at it and said, "NO! I didn't want chocolate!"

Holly woke up screaming in the night. She wasn't able to talk about it, until morning. She finally confided that she had a nightmare. I asked what the nightmare was about and she said, "The scary grown-up show." Ken and I reasoned that she must have been hearing, or seeing, some movie that we were watching, when we thought she was out of range. We were not sure what show it might have been. Holly repeatedly hit her forehead and said, "I can't get the bad thoughts out of my head!"

On subsequent nights, Holly complained of a recurring nightmare about *The Jungle Book* movie. We had owned the movie for years, and it had never bothered her before. When I asked her to tell me about the nightmare, she started crying and said, "You're not gonna like it!" Finally, she told me, "I told Sheer Khan that killing is bad. I'm sorry I said that word." Then she had a melt-down, crying inconsolably and repeating over and over, "I'm sorry; I'm so sorry!" I did my best to re-assure her that, although killing is bad, there is nothing inherently bad about using that word in a sentence.

The occupational therapist sent home a weighted vest for Holly to try wearing after dinner. It was supposed to have a calming effect, and perhaps help with the evening routine. Holly said it was for dress-up. She liked wearing it, but she kept taking the weights out. The next day, when I tried to put it on her, she said, "I already said I liked it; why are you putting it on again?"

CHAPTER NINETEEN

The next challenge in Holly's education was when her general education kindergarten teacher went on maternity leave. The substitute teacher seemed to frequently become frustrated with Holly. She and Holly did not get off to a great start together. The first day Holly refused to work for Mrs. Watson. She said, "Mrs. Watson is not my teacher." We had to explain to her that there are many teachers at her school and that she is expected to follow the directions of all teachers.

"She doesn't seem to be connecting with the other kids in the class," Mrs. Watson began telling me. "When it's indoor recess and I ask her who she wants to play with, she just looks around and decides what activity she wants to do and then goes there. It doesn't even seem to matter to her who the other kid is playing that game."

"You have stinky breath!" Holly told a classmate on a day I was visiting her kindergarten room.

"Hey!" the boy complained. "Holly said that I have stinky breath!"

"But he does have stinky breath," Holly justified.

Mrs. Watson called Holly over to her desk. "It's not polite to tell someone that he has stinky breath," she explained.

"But he does have stinky breath!" Holly stated more emphatically. She was beginning to get upset.

"Just because something is true," Mrs. Watson began in a hushed tone, "doesn't mean you have to say it. When you said that, you hurt his feelings. What could you have done instead?"

Holly shrugged.

"You could have just thought it in your head without saying it. You could have ignored the stinky breath or you could have moved away. Let's try to do one of those things next time. Now you can go back to your seat."

As she returned to her seat, she muttered under her breath, "I don't get why I got in trouble just because he has stinky breath!"

A few days later, Holly got in trouble for cutting in front of someone in line. "I was just doing what Mrs. Watson told me to do," she complained to me that evening.

"When did she ever tell you to cut in line?" I asked, confused.

"She said when Tony has stinky breath, I should move away from him. That's what I was trying to do when I got in trouble."

After a couple of weeks with Mrs. Watson, it was Holly's turn to be star student of the week. She was supposed to bring a poster with answers to various questions, such as "When is your birthday?" and "Who is in your family?" We completed the poster together, including several photos. Holly decorated the unused spaces of the poster board with drawings of unicorns.

When it was time for her to present the poster to her class, she said, "I started liking unicorns when I first heard about them and when I first saw one unicorn. Once I went to Walgreens and there were lots of things in there. Me and Mommy and Daddy and my sister Shelly went there because we had to get my dad's medicine, but we didn't want to go through the drive-through so we went inside. I discovered lots of things: medicine, shampoos and even toys. On one of the shelves, I saw a dog toy and a unicorn toy and I extremely wanted that unicorn toy because I was very interested in that toy up there and Shelly really wanted the dog toy so Mommy and Daddy got them both and when I looked at the unicorn, I saw the writings of a name 'Markie.' Then I took a closer look at its horn and its horn was very beautiful. Markie was a rainbow colored unicorn and that's how I started my collection of unicorns.

"I collect unicorns any time I get one. As the days went by, I became more and more interested in unicorns. One day I found a website on my computer called unicorns.com and I saw lots of unicorn things: unicorn legends, lots of pictures, unicorn t-shirts and even unicorn money. There was lots of stuff. I looked at the unicorn paintings and one of the paintings was very beautiful. One of them was under a rainbow. I really liked the stuff on that unicorn website and there were lots of books in my library; a few of them were about unicorns. One of the books told all about unicorns. And the book I was most interested in was the book called BEHOLD THE UNICORNS.

"Did you know that back when the people were writing the Bible story, they actually thought that an antelope was a unicorn? They really thought that! And now I know lots and lots about unicorns. But somehow I still wish I could learn more. And now I believe in unicorns because I know about them and I just really do believe in unicorns. It's kind of hard to explain how I became a lover of unicorns, but I can tell you this: I've got lots and lots of unicorn stuff in my room."

Mrs. Watson complained, "That wasn't the point of the star student assignment." It seemed to immensely frustrate her that Holly talked about unicorns all the time.

Holly began bringing school papers home with bold red letters saying "NO UNICORNS!"

I could tell that Mrs. Watson was getting frustrated at the intrusion of unicorns into all of Holly's school work, including math papers and poems about Christopher Columbus.

Holly did not care at all about the "NO UNICORNS" messages from her teacher. It was obvious that Mrs. Watson's notes were not going to change her unicorn habits. What was hardest for me was that I had spent my whole life trying to please teachers and now I had no idea how to help my daughter get back into her teacher's good graces. It was obvious that, with Holly, I could not expect or assume that every teacher would connect with her. I greatly appreciated the times when teachers saw past her challenges to appreciate her strengths, but I often felt almost like I needed to apologize for the extra work and patience she required.

"I met with Mrs. Watson to talk about Holly's unicorn situation," I told the school social worker, Mrs. Adams. "She says she gives Holly time to use unicorns if it is a creative assignment, such as creative writing or drawing. She doesn't allow unicorns for math because she says Holly turns a five minute math worksheet into a forty-five minute math assignment. She's obviously frustrated and I just don't know how to make her happy."

"Why do you think it's your job to make the teacher happy?" the social worker asked.

"Well," I fumbled, "I just like happy people." The truth was, I did not like conflict and I wanted everyone, including myself, the teacher and Holly to co-exist in peace.

A few days later, Holly rode home on the bus. "Did you hear me crying at school?" she asked.

"No, Honey!" I said. "I didn't hear you crying. I can't hear you when you're at school and I'm at home. Why were you crying?"

"When Mrs. Watson's fussing hits my eyes, it makes my eye water fall like onions do." She said.

"Why was Mrs. Watson fussing?" I asked.

"I was writing a paper about why I am special, but Mrs. Watson got mad and tore it up because I didn't ask to draw first. I was feeling sad inside and I hid under the table and Mrs. Watson said she isn't going to be my friend anymore," Holly said.

My heart sank. I felt horrible to know that Holly had had such a rough day. I was confused, saddened and angry about the remark that Mrs. Watson said she wasn't going to be her friend anymore. It seemed that it couldn't be true, but why would Holly say that?

The next day, I called Mrs. Watson to ask her perspective on the event. She said that she did tell Holly that it wasn't drawing time, but she didn't tear the picture. She did not understand why Holly suddenly got upset and hid under the table. "I did not say that I'm not going to be her friend anymore. I would never say that. I don't know why she would have said or even thought that!" she told me. "If it makes you feel any better, she is having a wonderful day at school today," she added.

In time, Holly and Mrs. Watson came to an understanding. Mrs. Watson began to appreciate that Holly had a sense of humor that was more mature than some of her peers. One child asked, "Where do I hand in my homework?

"Let's see," Mrs. Watson began, "where do we put our finished work? Does it go in my purse?"

"No!" Holly giggled.

"Do we put it in the trash?" Mrs. Watson asked.

"No!" Holly laughed.

"Well, where does it go then?" Mrs. Watson asked again.

"In the 'Finished Work' basket," Holly chuckled. Mrs. Watson was pleased at this interaction.

Mrs. Watson also began to notice, appreciate and encourage Holly's strengths. "If anyone in the class is having trouble with reading, Holly is one of our classroom reading experts. You can ask her and she can help you."

Just before Valentine's Day, Mrs. Watson asked, "Holly, could you teach me how to make a unicorn Valentine card?"

"It's no problem," Holly exclaimed. "First you draw a heart," she instructed, "then you draw a unicorn coming out of it." We had watched an artist on a video explain how to draw common objects and animals from basic shapes, such as circles, squares and triangles. For Holly, a unicorn was a basic shape.

One day Holly's back pack contained a unicorn chapter book. I was pleased, thinking that Mrs. Watson was trying to find another way to connect with Holly. After we read the book, Holly confessed that the book was part of the classroom library and she had put it in her back pack without permission. I recognized that Holly's unicorn obsession had led to her impulsive action of stashing the book in her bag. I knew that she only wanted to bring the book home so that I could read it to her; she wasn't meaning to "steal" it. I was glad that she had told me the truth. I wrote a note to Mrs. Watson explaining the situation and returning the book.

Later, I found out that Mrs. Watson had called Holly aside and asked her, "What is it called when you take something without permission?" Holly was terrified and would not answer. "It's called stealing!" Mrs. Watson told her. I worried about the conversation because I did not want Holly to begin to think of herself as a thief.

A few weeks later, Holly's backpack had another book in it that I did not recognize. I asked Holly where the book came from. She couldn't tell me. Finally, I asked her if it was a mistake and she said yes. I sent the book back to school with a note. Mrs. Watson sent a note in response which stated, "I should have written a note or double checked with Holly to make sure she understood. The book was a gift for 'March is Reading Month' for all the kids to keep."

At first, my caseload at school did not have any students with Autism. Before long, a student moved into our district and I began working with him. Next, a student with Autism who had been dually enrolled in an early childhood program and kindergarten exited the early childhood program and was placed on my caseload. The third student was referred to me and the school psychologist and school social worker for evaluation. It seemed strange to be a member of the multidisciplinary evaluation team for an Autism Spectrum Disorder after recently going through the process as a parent.

Over a short period of time, I had five students with Autism on my caseload. At that point, my supervisor invited me to attend a grant-supported Autism training through the STatewide Autism Resources and Training (START) Project. The first module I attended was called Behavioral Support for Students with Autism Spectrum Disorder.

I enthusiastically attended the training hoping that I would learn many strategies to help Holly, as well as my students. I was immediately impressed with the presenter's attitude. She expressed a respect and acceptance of students with autism that I had not previously encountered. She told story after story of teachers complaining about the behavior of students in their classrooms to which she responded, "What do you expect? He has Autism!" She further professed, "If you try to fight the Autism, you will always lose; you need to use the Autism to the student's advantage. The good news about students with Autism is that they are driven to their areas of interest. The bad news about students with Autism is that they are driven to their areas of interest." I began to think about Holly's unicorn pictures on her math papers and poems. It suddenly seemed to me that we were trying to fight the Autism. It also seemed to me that we were trying to "fix" her when she wasn't broken.

I was profoundly influenced by a quote by John Herner that was presented at the START training. "If a child doesn't know how to read, we teach. If a child doesn't know how to swim, we teach. If a child doesn't know how to multiply, we teach. If a child doesn't know how to behave, we punish?" The speaker encouraged positive behavior support to make the undesirable behavior non-effective and the positive behavior more effective.

"Your response should be non-emotional, non-verbal and non-punitive," she stated. I wondered what was left. She continued, "I often ask teachers, 'Why are you so angry that he can't be successful right now? If anything, we should be feeling sympathetic.'" The two day training went on to describe a problem-solving model resulting in an individual behavior support plan targeting one or two behaviors. "We need to change the problem-solving task from emotional to cognitive."

"Educators can be absurd sometimes," the speaker elaborated. "They find out something that a kid likes and they immediately want to make it contingent on some behavior. I'm always looking for 'what does he like and how can I give it to him and lots of it?' We want to teach him how to get his needs met appropriately."

The speaker cautioned against using the word "noncompliant" to describe students on the Autism spectrum. "That word assumes that the child is actively deciding not to do it. We should never rule out the possibility that it is a skill deficiency."

A teacher in the room asked a question related to her frustration with trying to get her student with ASD to achieve curriculum benchmarks. "I don't think he belongs in my class," she said. "He's never going to get it." The speaker began explaining that the primary purposes of education are to teach independence and socialization skills.

"You can know everything in the curriculum from kindergarten through twelfth grade, but if you don't have independence and social skills, you are unemployable," she said. "On the other hand, if you know nothing from the curriculum, but you have independence and social skills, there is something that you will be able to do."

The speaker also talked about the selective attention of students with ASD. She said that they are less likely to attend to and emulate adults than peers who are more similar to them. She emphasized the need for positive peer models.

After attending the START training, I began to work with Mrs. Wright in using Holly's unicorn obsession to teach her the curriculum requirements. We began giving her unicorn math problems, such as, "If three unicorns are in a field, how many legs are there? How many eyes are there? How many horns are there?"

Holly asked, "Mommy, wouldn't it be great if all math problems were unicorn math problems?"

We also talked to the students in Holly's class about her and about ASD. We asked them to tell us some of the ways that Holly was like them and some of the ways that she was different. We gave them honest answers to their questions about some of Holly's actions and difficulties. Then we implemented a program called "Friend for the Day." At the start of each afternoon of kindergarten, Holly would look at pictures of the students in her room and choose one to sit by her at circle time, line up next to her and play with her at recess.

At first I had some reservations about telling the other students about her ASD, but I realized that they already knew she was different. "If we don't teach them what to call it, they'll come up with something worse than Autism," Mrs. Watson said. The Friend for the Day program was surprisingly positive for Holly and all of her peer volunteers.

One morning, I was getting Holly ready for school. As I combed her hair, she vehemently protested. "Holly, I am trying to be gentle, but I'm also trying to hurry."

"It feels like you're more trying to hurry than trying to be gentle," she protested.

Due to my work schedule and Ken's work schedule, Holly and Shelly needed to go to daycare on some days after Holly got out of school. We were precise in letting the school know which days Holly would be picked up, which days she would ride the bus home and which days she would go to day care.

When there was a change to her schedule, I would inform the school by phone, email and written note. I would also make sure to remind Holly where she would be going after school. One day, she was supposed to ride the bus home. Ken saw the bus pass by the apartment building without stopping. Holly was not on the bus. Ken called the school and asked where Holly was. The secretary said she was in the office waiting to be picked up. After we questioned several people at the school, we learned that in addition to my phone call, email, and note in her backpack, Holly had told the substitute teacher that she was supposed to ride the bus home, but the substitute told her she was wrong. After that, we had to add an additional step of putting a tag on her backpack indicating where she would go after school.

"This is Nick, the bully from day care," Holly told me when I came to pick her up. I looked beyond Nick to the shocked expression of his mother's face. She was standing behind her son. Equally stunned, I did not know how to respond, so I remained silent.

"He's not the same bully as the bully from my class. That bully's name is Tony," Holly continued.

"Holly," I said in hushed tones, "It's not nice to call someone a bully."

"But he is a bully!" she asserted loudly. "Even Mrs. Watson knows he's a bully. She even said one day, 'Today is the day that the bullying is gonna stop!'"

One day, when I was visiting in Holly's kindergarten class, Mrs. Watson was reading the book CHICKA CHICKA BOOM BOOM to the class. We had read the book so many times at home; Holly and I both had it memorized. "A told B and B told C, I'll meet you at the top of the Coconut Tree...."[1]

As we were leaving school that day, Holly asked, "Mommy, do you think the letters wanted to eat the coconuts?" In all the hundreds of times I had read that book to her, I had never stopped to question the motivation of the alphabet letters in heading up the coconut tree.

One day, Holly told me, "I got a red slip in choir and I'm about to get kicked out of choir." My questions just increased her anxiety and did not clear anything up. I checked in Holly's backpack to see if there was a note of explanation. There were no notes from school. I checked email. Nothing. I checked voicemail. Nothing. I asked Ken if he had any idea what Holly was talking about. He hadn't heard anything from school. The next day, I called the music teacher. She said, "Holly must have misunderstood. She was never in any danger of being kicked out."

Mrs. Wright was in charge of a book swap at school. Every student was encouraged to bring in a used book to exchange for a used book that another student had donated. Mrs. Wright told me, "I put aside a unicorn book for Holly. As soon as I saw it, I knew I needed to save it for Holly because it was about unicorns, but don't tell anyone because she's the only student in the school that I saved a book for." I was touched that she was going out of her way to be kind to Holly; I was also once again aware of how much Holly stood out from the crowd.

Mrs. Wright sent me a note about her day. The note said that they were introducing a new science topic about plants. They brought the class

---

[1] CHICKA CHICKA BOOM BOOM by Bill Martin, Jr. and John Archambault

185

out to their school garden with various plants, and a pond with goldfish and turtles. They asked the children to raise their hands and tell things that they already knew about gardens. Many children contributed plant facts. Holly volunteered, "Never put a turtle in a hamster ball."

Mrs. Wright said that it was so cute the way her peers sat straight-faced as if thinking, "Good answer." The note ended with, "Ah, words to live by."

For Teacher Appreciation Day, I bought some chocolate turtle candies, and filled a hamster ball with them.

Holly saw it and objected, "Mommy! You know that's not right!"

I consoled her by saying, "It's okay, Holly. Your teachers will understand that it's kind of like a joke." Her teachers laughed until they cried, and said that was the funniest teacher gift they had ever received.

That evening, I had a smile on my face, as I plopped down in the recliner, and put my feet up. Holly and Shelly climbed onto my lap and I breathed in deeply the scent of their hair. It smelled even better than the baby-powder scented hair of my cabbage patch doll all those years ago.

"Mommy?" Holly said.

"Yes?"

"You make me feel very comfortable inside."

"You make me feel very comfortable inside too, Holly," I said, my heart feeling all warm and fuzzy.

"I love you more than a real live unicorn on earth," Holly said quietly.

Well, she stumped me again. How could I top that compliment? Proud and happy to be defeated, I simply hugged the two soft, warm treasures on my lap and said, "I love you both so, so much, forever and ever, Amen!"

Made in the USA